from creation to

new creation

Making sense of the whole Bible story

Tim Chester

From Creation to New Creation
Making sense of the whole Bible story

This revised 2nd edition © Tim Chester 2010
Originally published in 2003

Published by
The Good Book Company
Tel (UK): 0333–123–0880;
International: +44 (0) 208 942 0880
Email: admin@thegoodbook.co.uk

Websites:
UK: www.thegoodbook.co.uk
N America: www.thegoodbook.com
Australia: www.thegoodbook.com.au
New Zealand: www.thegoodbook.co.nz

ISBN: 9781907377341

Cover design: Steve Devane
Illustrations: André Parker
Printed in the UK

Contents

Acknowledgements

This book began life as a series of seminars at Spring Harvest Word Alive 2002 and as a training course for Kev and Ruth Gookey, missionaries with Radstock Ministries to Albania. I want to express my thanks to Angela Taylor, Ken Armstrong, Lyssa Bode, Peter Comont, Richard Chester and Steve Timmis, who all made valuable comments on the manuscript.

Thank you, too, to the Good Book Company for giving the book a new lease of life in this second edition. Thanks especially to Tim Thornborough for his editorial work and André Parker for the illustrations.

The book is dedicated to my daughters, Katie and Hannah, with the prayer that they will grow to love this story as much as I do.

Introduction

I was visiting some Jewish friends. The wife teaches in the sabbath school at the local synagogue. I picked up a commentary on the Torah (the first five books of the Bible) and started flicking through it. She enthused about the commentary and asked what I thought. I said: "It's a bit like hearing a joke without the punchline. It's missing the point of the Torah, which is Jesus Christ." My friends know that Christians believe Jesus is the promised Messiah. But they were surprised by my response. "What?" they said. "You believe *all* the Bible points to Jesus?"

John 5 v 39-40
"You diligently study the Scriptures because you think that by them you possess eternal life. These are the Scriptures that testify about me, yet you refuse to come to me to have life."

The Scriptures, says Jesus, are about Him.

Luke 24 v 25-27, 44-47
He said to them, "How foolish you are, and how slow of heart to believe all that the prophets have spoken! Did not the Christ have to suffer these things and then enter his glory?"

And beginning with Moses and all the Prophets, he explained to them what was said in all the Scriptures concerning himself.

Figure 1: The Hebrew Bible and the English Bible

The English Bible

History		Wisdom	Prophecy
Law	History		
Genesis to Deuteronomy	Joshua to Esther	Job to Song of Solomon	Isaiah to Malachi

The Hebrew Bible

The Law	The Prophets		The Writings
	Former	Latter	
Genesis to Deuteronomy	Joshua to 1 and 2 Kings (minus Ruth)	Isaiah to Malachi (minus Lam and Dan)	Ps, Job, Prov, Ruth, Song, Ecc. Lam, Esther, Dan, Ezra, Neh, 1 and 2 Chron.

He said to them, "This is what I told you while I was still with you: Everything must be fulfilled that is written about me in the Law of Moses, the Prophets and the Psalms."

Then he opened their minds so they could understand the Scriptures. He told them, "This is what is written: The Christ will suffer and rise from the dead on the third day, and repentance and forgiveness of sins will be preached in his name to all nations, beginning at Jerusalem."

The Hebrew Bible is arranged differently from the Old Testament in our English bibles (see Figure 1). So when Jesus says: "Everything must be fulfilled that is written about me in the Law of Moses, the Prophets and the Psalms" (Luke 24 v 44), He is talking about the Old Testament ("the Psalms" was often used as a shorthand for all the books in the section called the Writings).

Jesus explains how "all the Scriptures" are about Him. What is written in the Scriptures is this: "The Christ will suffer and rise from the dead on the third day, and repentance and forgiveness of sins will be preached in his name to all nations, beginning at Jerusalem" (Luke 24 v 46-47). On the first Easter Day the risen Christ expounds the Scriptures. He shows that all the Old Testament points to Him: His death, His resurrection and His proclamation to the nations. It is not just that there are a few messianic prophecies dotted around. The whole Bible is about Jesus, from beginning to end.

Most people read detective novels from beginning to end, pitting their wits against the author, trying to pick up the clues and work out who did it. But some people like to read the last chapter first. They want to know from the beginning how it will end. Then, as they read the rest of the book, it makes sense straight away. As Christians we should read the Bible—and especially the Old Testament—in this second way. We should read it at all times through Jesus Christ, so that we can make sense of it as we go along.

There are two implications of this:

We need Christ to understand the Bible

Christ is the key that unlocks the meaning of the Scriptures. The Bible makes sense as we see it focused on Him. This especially needs to be said of the Old Testament. We can only understand the Old Testament when we see how it points to Jesus. Jesus gives the Bible meaning. Thinking about how Jesus fulfils the promises and story of the Old Testament enables us to read the Old Testament as Christians.

We need the Old Testament to understand Christ

The New Testament writers understood Jesus in Old Testament categories. They wrote of Christ as the fulfiller of the Old Testament. We can only fully understand who Jesus is and what He has done as we understand the Old Testament background that the New Testament writers drew upon to explain Him.

Biblical theology is the term used for this approach to the Bible. The term can be used in a wide sense to mean theology that is based on, and true to, the Bible. But it is also used in a narrower sense to mean looking at how the Bible fits together. It enables us to see how the parts relate to the whole. Without a sense of the whole—of the overall plan of salvation—we will find it hard to understand the parts. And by understanding the whole we grow in our understanding of who God is, what He has done and what He will do. We grow in our understanding of our place within those purposes. Biblical theology gives us a biblical worldview. Maybe sometimes we wish the Bible was written in the form of an encyclopaedia of theology and ethics in which we could look up God under "g" and prayer under "p". But it is not: it is a story. Understanding the story is the only way to understand the Bible and its theology. It is the way the New Testament writers used the Old Testament.

Biblical theology also safeguards us from two common ways of *mis*reading the Bible, especially the Old Testament— allegorising and moralising.

Allegorising

Allegorising, or spiritualising, is reading a meaning into a passage from outside. Characters or events are said to represent "spiritual" truths. Allegorising bypasses the plain meaning of the words and looks instead for hidden meanings. An example is seeing David's defeat of Goliath as a model for Christians, who fight against their "giants" with the "stones" of prayer, faith and so on. The meaning we give to the "stones" in this instance is ultimately arbitrary. The problem with this is that the Bible can be made to mean anything at the whim of the reader. But God has not **hidden** truth in the Bible, but **revealed** it in a way that is open to all.

Moralising

Moralising sees the stories of the Old Testament as moral tales written to instruct us. The problem with this is that they are often immoral tales with morally complex characters. It is often unclear whether the actions of a character are a good or bad example to us. Jephthah, for example, vows to sacrifice the first thing he sees on his return from victory, but the first thing he sees is his daughter (Judges 11). Is Jephthah a warning against rash promises or an example of devotion of God? In order to decide we employ, at best, principles from elsewhere in Scripture and, at worst, our own prejudice. In reality, the story of the Old Testament is first and foremost God's story. Moralising bypasses Christ, reducing the message of the Bible to a message of moral rectitude rather than a message of salvation and grace. It is not the case that salvation is gained by obeying the law in the Old Testament and by faith in Christ in the New Testament. The message of the Bible from start to finish is that salvation is by grace.

Both allegorising and moralising involve reading into the text of Scripture something from outside. As a result we do not hear the word of God, but some other voice. Even at its best—when it is New Testament truth read into the

Old Testament—it does not allow us to hear the authentic voice of the Old Testament as it witnesses to Christ. As a result our understanding and appreciation of Christ are impoverished.

The story of a promise

The Bible is the story of God's salvation. Genesis 1 – 3 describes how God made the world good and made humanity to enjoy His world. He placed us under His good rule—a rule that brought life and freedom. But humanity rejected God's rule and incurred God's wrath. The rest of the Bible is the story of how God sets about restoring what was lost and fulfilling His purposes in creation. At the heart of that is a promise.

Genesis 12 v 1-7
The LORD had said to Abram, "Leave your country, your people and your father's household and go to the land I will show you.

"I will make you into a great nation and I will bless you; I will make your name great, and you will be a blessing. I will bless those who bless you, and whoever curses you I will curse; and all peoples on earth will be blessed through you."

So Abram left, as the LORD had told him; and Lot went with him. Abram was seventy-five years old when he set out from Haran. He took his wife Sarai, his nephew Lot, all the possessions they had accumulated and the people they had acquired in Haran, and they set out for the land of Canaan, and they arrived there.

Abram travelled through the land as far as the site of the

great tree of Moreh at Shechem. At that time the Canaanites were in the land. The LORD appeared to Abram and said, "To your offspring I will give this land." So he built an altar there to the LORD, who had appeared to him.

There are three core elements to this promise:

1. A people who know God
"I will make you into a great nation and I will bless you; I will make your name great, and you will be a blessing" (Genesis 12 v 2).

2. A land of blessing
"The LORD appeared to Abram and said, 'To your offspring I will give this land'" (Genesis 12 v 7).

3. Blessing to the nations
"I will bless those who bless you, and whoever curses you I will curse; and all peoples on earth will be blessed through you" (Genesis 12 v 3).

Some people see the promise to Abraham as a people, a land and blessing. While we can view the patterns of biblical theology differently, it seems to me that the emphasis falls on the nations as the third element of the promise. "Blessing" in the context of Genesis has specific content. It is blessing in the face of the curse God has declared on creation. The fall led to a curse and now God promises a blessing. He promises, in other words, to reverse the judgment brought about by humanity's disobedience. The promise of blessing is a promise to rescue us from sin and judgment. The promise of a people is part of that rescue: a people alienated from God and one another will become a new humanity who are God's people. The promise of a land is also part of that promise: we will return to a place of blessing in a restored Eden. The promise of blessing is not additional to the promise of a people and a land, for the blessing consists in being the people who know God in the place blessed by God. The additional element, therefore, is that this blessing will extend to all peoples.

There is one further element to add.

4. A King and a kingdom

This promise of a King and a kingdom runs throughout the Bible. It is anticipated in the promise to Abraham. In Genesis 12 God promises Abraham not simply a people but "a nation"—a word that describes a political entity. God says to Abraham: "I will make nations of you, and kings will come from you" (Genesis 17 v 6). But this element of the promise of salvation comes in a new and distinctive way to David.

2 Samuel 7 v 11-16

"'The LORD declares to you that the LORD himself will establish a house for you: When your days are over and you rest with your fathers, I will raise up your offspring to succeed you, who will come from your own body, and I will establish his kingdom. He is the one who will build a house for my Name, and I will establish the throne of his kingdom for ever. I will be his father, and he shall be my son. When he does wrong, I will punish him with the rod of men, with floggings inflicted by men. But my love will never be taken away from him, as I took it away from Saul, whom I removed from before you. Your house and your kingdom shall endure for ever before me; your throne shall be established for ever.'"

The promises—or different dimensions to the one promise of salvation—drive the Bible story. The promises are affirmed in covenants with Abraham, with Moses, with David and in the new covenant that Christ makes. A covenant is a formally agreed promise—a "contract", we might say today. There are different covenants, but underlying them is one promise.

Galatians 3 v 8
The Scripture foresaw that God would justify the Gentiles by faith, and announced the gospel in advance to Abraham: "All nations will be blessed through you."

Paul says that the promise to Abraham is the gospel announced in advance. The promise that was made to Abraham is the same promise that comes to us in the gospel.

The Bible is the story of how God fulfils this promise to Abraham. The Old Testament is the story of how God partially fulfils the promise in the life of Israel. But each partial fulfilment points to its ultimate fulfilment through Jesus. And along the way the promise gets bigger because God's ultimate purposes are for a new humanity in a new creation. The promise is fulfilled *through* Jesus and *in* the new creation.

In the rest of this book we are going to trace each of these elements of the promise of salvation through the Bible.

This book can be read in two ways. You can read about each element of the promise in turn, tracing it through the Bible (reading vertically down Figure 2). Alternatively you can read about each stage in the Bible story, exploring what is happening to the promise of salvation at that point in the story (reading horizontally across Figure 2). To help you do

Figure 2: Summary

	A people who know God	A place of blessing	A king and a kingdom	Blessing to the nations
Creation (Gen. 1 – 2)	Humanity with God	At home in Eden	God rules through His word	Commanded to fill the earth
Fall (Gen. 3 – 11)	Humanity alienated	Expelled from Eden	God's rule rejected	The nations against God
Abraham (Gen. 12 – 50)	A people promised	A land promised	God rules through His covenant promise	Promised blessings to all nations
Israel (Ex. – Kings)	A people set free	A land given with Jerusalem and temple	God rules through His king	Called to draw the nations to God's rule
Decline into exile (2 Kings)	A people in captivity	A land lost, Jerusalem and temple destroyed	God rules through the prophetic word	Drawn to the ways of the nations
Prophecy	A remnant people	A land to be restored with a new Jerusalem	God will rule through a coming king	Judgment and salvation will come to the nations
Jesus	JESUS			
The church	A new people	Blessing in Christ and God's living temple	King Jesus rules through the gospel	The gospel to all nations
New creation	A new humanity	A new creation	God's everlasting rule of freedom	People from every nation

this each chapter uses the same headings (the headings in first column of Figure 2).

The aim of this book is to give you a sense of how the different elements of God's promise of salvation unfold. This in turn will enable you to begin to read the Bible as a whole and see how it applies to us as Christians today. As you read a passage of the Bible ask yourself the following questions:

- What is happening to each element of the promise at this point in the story?
- What does this story tell us about God and His rule?
- How does this section contrast with, point to or illuminate the work of Christ?
- How does this section give us confidence in the word of promise that comes to us in the gospel?
- What does this section tell us about how people are to respond to the word of promise?

At the end of each chapter I have tried to sketch out how this might be done, using the book of Nehemiah as a case study to illustrate the principles involved.

But before we begin to explore how the promise of salvation unfolds, we must get an overview of the Bible story. If you are already familiar with the story of the Bible, you might want to skip the next chapter and go on to Chapter Two.

Chapter 1

The story of the promise of salvation

I remember well the first time I saw a diagram like Figure 3. It blew my mind. I had thought of the Bible as a fragmented collection of largely unrelated stories. Perhaps they combined to give us a picture of God. Perhaps they gave us moral examples to follow. But now, suddenly, and for the first time, I saw that the Bible was one story. All the separate stories were episodes in one whole. And what is more, far from being a collection of moral examples, this was the story of salvation. The hero of the big story—and every episode within the big story—was not Moses, David, Elijah or Paul, but God Himself.

This story is not only the story of the Bible. It is the story of human history. In cultures all over the world people tell stories. Some are narrated by a storyteller; today many are in the form of books, films and television programmes. Some stories are fictional, while some are true, but all of them have the potential to shape our worldview. Societies pass on their values as they retell stories from their history. But all histories are in reality part of the one story that the Bible narrates. This is the story that makes sense of the world in which we live. This is the story that provides a true account of humanity and the world. This is the story that offers hope for the future. It is the story of God's promise to rescue people from sin and death.

Figure 3: An outline of the Bible story

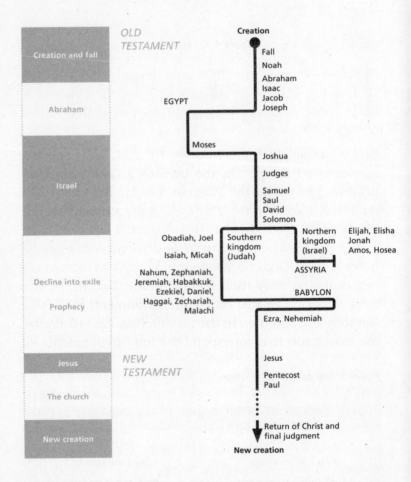

Creation

The Bible begins with God. Its opening words are "In the beginning God..." (Genesis 1 v 1). Before anything else began, God was. God is the eternally present being. "Before the mountains were born or you brought forth the earth and the world, from everlasting to everlasting you are God" (Psalm 90 v 2).

Figure 4: Creation

God is not only before all things, He made all things and rules over all things. "In the beginning God created the heavens and the earth" (Genesis 1 v 1). The world God made was a good world. Throughout the story of creation we are told: "God saw that it was good" (Genesis 1 v 10, 12, 18, 21, 25, 31). Out of what was "formless and empty" (Genesis 1 v 2) God created something that was ordered and beautiful. The story itself highlights this fact. In the first three days God created different environments from what was formless, and then in the second three days He created the inhabitants that correspond to those environments.

Figure 5: The pattern of creation

Forming what was formless	Filling what was empty
Day 1: Light	Day 4: Lights
Day 2: Waters and sky	Day 5: Fish and birds
Day 3: Ground and vegetation	Day 6: Animals and people

God created humanity in His image (Genesis 1 v 26-27). Being made in the image of God means we were made:

- to share God's rule over creation—God says: "Let them rule"
- to have relationships—God says: "Let us make man in our image", and He makes us "male and female" .

We were made to know God and enjoy a relationship with Him. God placed the first man and woman in a garden. It was a place of security and provision (Genesis 2 v 8-9).

God made the world through His word (Genesis 1 v 3, 6, 9, 11, 14, 20, 24). God rules through His word. We are made to live under the good rule of God—a rule that brings security, freedom and life. The first man and woman, Adam and Eve, were to express their commitment to God's rule through trust in the word of God:

Genesis 2 v 16-17

And the LORD God commanded the man, "You are free to eat from any tree in the garden; but you must not eat from the tree of the knowledge of good and evil, for when you eat of it you will surely die."

On the seventh day of creation God rested. So far each day had ended in the same way: "And there was evening, and there was morning—the first day" (Genesis 1 v 5, 8, 13, 19, 23, 31). But there is no such phrase for the seventh day. This is a day without end. This is the climax of creation. The world was created to share in the sabbath of God. God was not tired out. Rather, His work was done. It was not deficient in any way. "God saw all that he had made, and it was very good" (Genesis 1 v 31). But the good world that God made is no longer good. We see much in our world that is beautiful, good and true. But we also see evil, suffering and ugliness. Something has changed. Something has gone wrong.

Figure 6: The fall

The fall

Adam and Eve did not trust God's word or obey His command. Satan, in the form a serpent, came to Eve and questioned God's word. He made Adam and Eve doubt the goodness of God's rule (Genesis 3 v 1-5). They disobeyed God's command, and in so doing, they rejected His rule (Genesis 3 v 6-7). The order of creation had been subverted. God was to rule over people who were to rule over creation. Now the serpent controlled people who rejected God's authority.

Satan offered Adam and Eve the knowledge of "good and evil" (Genesis 3 v 5). This does not mean knowing *about* good and evil—they already knew that they should not eat of the tree of the knowledge of good and evil. Nor does it mean *experiencing* good and evil, since God Himself knows good and evil (Genesis 3 v 22). What it means is *determining* for oneself what is good and what is evil. It means deciding what is right—creating our own morality. Adam and Eve decided to live their lives their own way, without God. This is what defines sin. Sin is doubting the word of God and choosing to live our lives without God. In effect we knock God off His throne and put ourselves in His place. We decide to be gods for ourselves.

The result was catastrophic—not just for Adam and Eve, but for all of humanity and for all of creation.

Instead of life there is death

Adam and Eve were cut off from the tree of life. Although they did not die straight away, decay and frustration became part of human existence, which now ends in physical death. But worse still, we are condemned to eternal death, separated from the presence of God.

Instead of relationships there is hostility

Immediately Adam and Eve realised they were naked (Genesis 3 v 7). They were no longer at ease with themselves and each other. They hid from God. God was no longer a friend, but feared.

Instead of blessing there is curse

The world God made was a good world—a world of blessing. But now God has cursed the land. It will only provide through sweat and toil. Childbearing has become an experience of pain. Above all, humanity is under the curse of God's judgment. God is sovereign. He will rule. If we reject that rule, then we will experience His rule as judgment and defeat.

We call humanity's rejection of God "the fall". We fell into temptation and sin, and in so doing, we fell from life, relationship and blessing into death, hostility and curse. I once asked a group of international students whether the world is a happy place or a sad place. They could not agree. The evidence for both is compelling. On the one hand, the world is a place of great beauty, in which people enjoy wonderful food, tell jokes, create works of art, fall in love and so on. On the other hand, the world is a place of suffering and decay, conflict and heartbreak, frustration and thwarted ambition. The Bible story makes sense of these contrasting experiences. God made the world and the world He made was good. Much of that goodness is still present in the world. But humanity has rejected God's rule. We live without God and under God's curse. The result is conflict and suffering.

Adam and Eve's first two sons were Cain and Abel. Both offered sacrifices to God, but only Abel's was acceptable. In his jealousy Cain killed Abel (Genesis 4). The effect and extent of sin was becoming clear.

The Lord was so grieved over the extent of sin in the world that He decided to wipe humanity from the earth with a great flood (Genesis 6 – 9). Only Noah found favour (grace) in God's sight. God told Noah to build a large boat—an ark. Noah warned the people of God's impending judgment, but they mocked him. When the ark was finished, it rained for 40 days until water covered the entire earth. Only Noah and his family, together with representatives of all the animals, were saved.

Yet the wickedness of humanity continued. The people of the earth gathered together on the plain of Shinar, even though God had commanded them to scatter and fill the earth (Genesis 11). They began to build a tower up to heaven in defiance of God. They wanted to make a name for themselves. But their plans fell apart when God created confusion by causing them to speak different languages. The tower became known as Babel, which means "confusion".

But as the effects of sin became clear and the judgment

of God was revealed, there was hope. After the fall God said to the serpent: "And I will put enmity between you and the woman, and between your offspring and hers; he will crush your head, and you will strike his heel" (Genesis 3 v 15). A descendent of Adam and Eve will triumph through suffering. The serpent will strike His heel, but ultimately He will defeat Satan and bring hope to humanity. The work of Satan will be undone. He will be overthrown. Genesis 5 lists the descendants of Adam. This matters because one of Adam's descendants is going to defeat Satan. As the story progresses we are constantly asking: Who is this promised deliverer?

The flood is a picture of judgment, but Noah's ark is also a picture of salvation (1 Peter 3 v 18-22). It shows us that God saves people from judgment. When the flood waters had subsided and Noah could once again walk on the earth, God made a covenant with him. God promised that He would never again destroy the world through a flood. He gave the rainbow as a perpetual sign of this covenant.

Abraham
The people of Babel wanted to make a name for themselves. Soon afterwards God came to a man called Abram and promised that He would make his name great. God told

Figure 7: Abraham

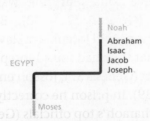

Abram—or Abraham as God renamed him—to leave his home in Ur and set out for a new land that God would give him (Genesis 12 and 15). God promised Abraham that his descendants would become a great nation, and that from them the Saviour would come. God promised Abraham that through him blessing would come to all nations. The fall of humanity into sin brought a curse, but now God promises blessing instead of curse.

As we look in the story for the deliverer promised to Adam, we know now to look within the family of Abraham. As Paul points out: "The promises were spoken to Abraham and to his seed. The Scripture does not say 'and to seeds', meaning many people, but "and to your seed", meaning one person ..." (Galatians 3 v 16). Throughout the Old Testament story we are asking: Who is the one offspring through whom the blessing of salvation will come?

Though Abraham's wife, Sarah, was old and barren, God gave them a son, who was named Isaac (Genesis 21). Isaac had twin sons—Esau and Jacob (Genesis 25). Esau was the firstborn and the inheritor of the promise, but Esau cared little for the promise of God. On one occasion he "sold" his birthright to Jacob for a bowl of stew (Genesis 25). As Isaac approached death, he called for Esau to prepare a meal at which Isaac would give him his blessing. But while Esau was out hunting, Jacob deceived his blind father, and received the blessing instead of Esau (Genesis 27).

Jacob had twelve sons, but one was his particular favourite—Joseph (Genesis 29 – 30). Because of their jealousy, the other sons sold Joseph as a slave into Egypt and told their father that they had found Joseph's bloodstained clothes in the desert (Genesis 37). Joseph ended up in prison in Egypt (Genesis 39). In prison he correctly interpreted the dreams of two of Pharaoh's top officials (Genesis 40). When

Pharaoh was troubled by a dream, Joseph was called for. He revealed that the dream was a prediction of seven years of plenty, followed by seven years of famine (Genesis 41). He advised Pharaoh to store up the excess during the good years in readiness for the lean years. Pharaoh was so impressed by Joseph that he made him second-in-command in Egypt.

As the years of famine dragged on, Jacob and his family faced starvation. Jacob was forced to send his sons to Egypt in search of food (Genesis 42 – 43), where they came before none other than their brother Joseph (Genesis 44). The family came to live in Egypt with the blessing of the Pharaoh (Genesis 45 – 46). The family from whom the Saviour would come was saved from famine by the remarkable providence of God. "You intended to harm me," said Joseph to his brothers, "but God intended it for good to accomplish what is now being done, the saving of many lives" (Genesis 50 v 20).

As we read the stories of conflict and tension within the families of Abraham, Isaac and Jacob, we are not simply reading a family saga. We are searching for the promised deliverer. We are tracing the hand of God as He fulfils His saving purposes. The structure of the book of Genesis brings this out. The material in Genesis has been arranged around a repeated phrase: "These are the generations of…" (ESV) or "This is the account of …" (NIV) (Genesis 2 v 4; 5 v 1; 6 v 9; 10 v 1; 11 v 10;11 v 27; 25 v 12, 19; 36 v 1, 9; 37 v 2). This is called the Toledoth formula, after the phrase in the original Hebrew language.

Tracing the story of Genesis through the Toledoth formula reveals God's election in action (see Figure 8). God is making choices. He is guiding the story towards the coming of the Saviour. He is choosing the line to whom the promise of salvation passes and from whom the Saviour will come. He

Figure 8: The structure of the book of Genesis

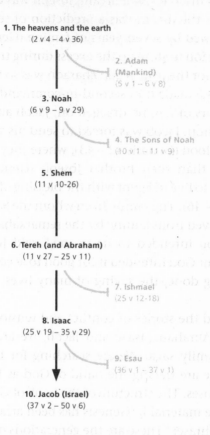

1. The heavens and the earth
(2 v 4 – 4 v 36)

2. Adam
(Mankind)
(5 v 1 – 6 v 8)

3. Noah
(6 v 9 – 9 v 29)

4. The Sons of Noah
(10 v 1 – 11 v 9)

5. Shem
(11 v 10-26)

6. Tereh (and Abraham)
(11 v 27 – 25 v 11)

7. Ishmael
(25 v 12-18)

8. Isaac
(25 v 19 – 35 v 29)

9. Esau
(36 v 1 – 37 v 1)

10. Jacob (Israel)
(37 v 2 – 50 v 6)

chooses Shem from among the sons of Noah. He chooses Isaac and not Ishmael. He chooses Jacob and not Esau. And He does not make these choices on merit, but on the basis of electing grace.

The structure of Genesis reveals a movement from humanity as a whole to the nation of Israel. The name "Adam" is a play on the Hebrew word for "mankind". The Adam section ends with the rejection of humanity and the declaration of God's intention to destroy humanity in a flood (Genesis 6 v 5-8). The book of Genesis ends with the section on Jacob—or "Israel", as he is renamed—and his sons, who form the tribes of the nation of Israel. The question of where the Saviour will come from has a partial answer: He will come from the nation of Israel.

The rise of Israel

As the generations passed, the family of Jacob grew into a nation—the nation of Israel. The Pharaohs of Egypt forgot the role of Joseph and enslaved the Israelites. Fearing the might of the Israelite nation, Pharaoh ordered that all newborn male children be drowned (Exodus 1). One Israelite family placed its child in a basket and floated him down the Nile in the hope that somehow he might be saved (Exodus 2). Under the hand of God, he was found by one of the daughters of Pharaoh, who decided to take the child as her own. The child's name was Moses.

For 40 years Moses lived as a son of Egypt until one day he saw an Egyptian mistreating an Israelite slave. In his anger he killed the Egyptian and was forced to flee for his

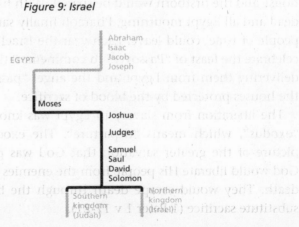

Figure 9: Israel

life to Midian (Exodus 2). In Midian he became a shepherd for 40 years, until one day he saw a bush that appeared to be burning, but which was not consumed (Exodus 3). From the bush God spoke to him. God said He had heard the cries of His people and had remembered His promise to Abraham. He was to send Moses to call on Pharaoh to let His people go.

Moses went to Pharaoh and told him to let God's people go (Exodus 5 and 7). When Pharaoh refused, God sent terrible plagues on Egypt (Exodus 7 – 10). Each challenged the power of the Egyptian gods. God was proving Himself to be the one true God. After each plague, Pharaoh relented, but then changed his mind. The tenth and final plague was the worst—God was going to send an angel of death to kill all the firstborn in the land (Exodus 11). God had promised Abraham that "whoever curses you I will curse" (Genesis 12 v 2-3). The Pharaoh who had tried to kill the children of Israel found his curse rebounding on his own people. The Israelites would only be spared by daubing the blood of a sacrificed lamb on their doorposts (Exodus 12). When the angel of death saw the blood, it would pass over that house and the firstborn would be spared. With his own son dead and all Egypt mourning, Pharaoh finally said that the people of Israel could leave. Each year the Israelites would celebrate the feast of "Passover" in commemoration of God delivering them from Egypt and the angel "passing over" the houses protected by the blood of sacrifice.

The liberation from slavery in Egypt was known as the "exodus", which means "departure". The exodus was a picture of the greater salvation that God was promising. God would liberate His people from the enemies of sin and death. They would escape death through the blood of a substitute sacrifice (1 Peter 1 v 17-21).

The Israelites set off into the desert. But once again Pharaoh changed his mind and marched out in pursuit (Exodus 14). Caught between the approaching Egyptian army and the Red Sea, there seemed no hope. But God told Moses to stretch out his staff over the Red Sea. As Moses did so, the waters parted and the Israelites were able to cross through the sea in safety. When the Egyptians followed, the waters closed again, and the army was drowned. God had saved His people. The future of the people from whom the promised deliverer would come had been safeguarded once again.

Guiding them by a pillar of cloud during the day and a pillar of fire at night (Exodus 13), God led His people to Mount Sinai so that they might meet with Him. When the people were hungry, God provided food called "manna" from heaven (Exodus 16). When the people were thirsty, He provided water from a rock (Exodus 17).

On Mount Sinai God made a covenant with His people. He promised to be their God and He called on them to obey Him. He gave them the Ten Commandments, inscribed on tablets of stone, along with other regulations (Exodus 20 – 31, Leviticus and Deuteronomy). If they lived under His rule, they would experience life in the land as a life of blessing and security. God provided the design for a "tabernacle"—a kind of portable temple. This would symbolise God's presence with His people. It was also the place where animals could be sacrificed. Again, animal sacrifice was a picture of salvation. Sin could only be dealt with through the death of a substitute.

But while Moses was with God on the mountain, the people grew restless. They asked Moses' brother, Aaron, to build a golden calf for them to worship (Exodus 32). God was revealing Himself through His word, but they wanted an image they could worship. Because of this idolatry, God said that, while He would bring the people to the land, His presence would not go with them. This was not enough for Moses. Moses realised that salvation was to know God's presence. He interceded with God and God answered his prayer (Exodus 33).

God led the people to the edge of the land He had promised to give them. But they were full of doubt, so they sent twelve spies into the land (Numbers 13). Ten of the spies said that the people were too fearsome for the Israelites to conquer. Only two of the spies, Joshua and Caleb, believed that God could give them the land. But the people did not listen to Joshua and Caleb. They did not trust the promise of God (Numbers 14). And so God said that the entire generation that had come out of the Egypt—with the exception of Joshua and Caleb—would not enter the land. They would wander in the desert for 40 years until they had died out. It would be their children who would enter the land.

And so it was. 40 years later, with Joshua in charge, it was the next generation that crossed the River Jordan and entered the land (Joshua 1 – 4). They were able to take the land because God fought for them (Joshua 6; 8; 10 – 12). On one occasion they attacked the heavily fortified city of Jericho (Joshua 6). God told them to march round the city each day for six days. On the seventh day they marched round seven times. At the end of the seventh circuit, as they sounded their trumpets, the walls of the city collapsed. There could be no doubt: the land was God's gift (Joshua 21 v 43-45).

But Israel did not dislodge all the inhabitants of the land as God had told them to (Judges 1). The generation that followed Joshua forgot the ways of God (Judges 2). They turned from God and so God delivered them over to their enemies. Oppressed in this way, they turned back to God, and God delivered them. The saviours that God sent to deliver the people were known as judges. While they led the people, the nation enjoyed a time of peace. But when they died, time and again the people turned from God. And so the cycle was repeated (see Figure 10), except that each time things were worse than before. The people were not so much circling round as spiralling down into moral and political chaos.

Figure 10: The cycle of the judges

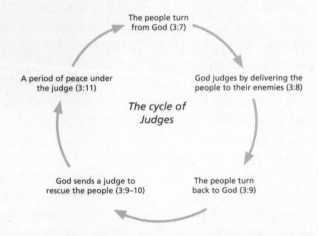

The best-known judges are probably Deborah, Gideon, Samson and Samuel. Deborah was a prophetess who judged the nation and rescued the people from the Canaanites (Judges 4 – 5). Gideon delivered the people with just 300 men, demonstrating that it was God who was the true Judge (Judges 6 – 7). Samson was given unparalleled strength by God as long as his hair remained uncut (Judges 13 – 16). But Samson had a weakness for foreign women and one named Delilah deceived him into revealing the secret of his strength. His hair was cut and he was captured by Israel's enemies, the Philistines. God granted him one last, poignant act of strength as he was paraded in the temple of the Philistines. He brought down the central pillars on himself and all those inside.

The last of the judges was Samuel. Samuel was born in response to the desperate prayers for a child of his mother, Hannah (1 Samuel 1-2). As she had vowed before God, Hannah dedicated Samuel to the service of God, and he grew up in the tabernacle at Shiloh. During Samuel's time the people asked for a king like the other nations had (1 Samuel 8). Though Samuel warned them that they were rejecting God as their King, and that a king would oppress them, the people persisted, and God granted their request by giving them Saul as king (1 Samuel 9 – 10). Saul started well, but soon he departed from the ways of the Lord (1 Samuel 15), and so Samuel anointed a young shepherd boy, David, instead (1 Samuel 16). David proved his trust in God early in life by defeating the giant Goliath with his slingshot (1 Samuel 17). Saul grew jealous and fearful of David and David spent many years as a fugitive from Saul (1 Samuel 19 – 30). Nevertheless, when Saul died in battle, David became king (2 Samuel 1 – 5).

David was Israel's greatest king. He captured Jerusalem and made it the capital of the nation (2 Samuel 5). He extended the borders and subjugated the surrounding nations (2 Samuel 8). God made a covenant with David in which He promised that one of David's descendants would rule over God's people for ever (2 Samuel 7). We knew that deliverance for humanity would come from a descendant of Adam. Then we found that the deliverer would be a descendant of Abraham. Now we discover that we must look within the family of David for God's promised Saviour-King.

David himself was not the promised Saviour. He committed adultery with a woman named Bathsheba (2 Samuel 11 – 12). When she conceived, he arranged for her husband to be killed. In judgment God said: "The sword shall never depart from your house" (2 Samuel 12 v 10). David's first son, Amnon, raped his half-sister (2 Samuel 13) and was murdered by another son, Absalom. Absalom himself usurped David for a period of time, forcing David into temporary exile (2 Samuel 13 – 18).

David was finally succeeded by Solomon (1 Kings 1 – 2). God offered Solomon whatever he wanted and Solomon chose wisdom (1 Kings 3). People from around the world came to marvel at Solomon's wisdom and his reign was one of plenty (1 Kings 10). Solomon built a permanent temple for God in Jerusalem. This was the high point of the nation of Israel. But in Solomon's reign the seeds of decline were sown. Solomon took many foreign wives, who turned his

Figure 11: Decline into Exile and the rise of prophecy

Samuel
Saul
David
Solomon

Obadiah, Joel	Southern kingdom (Judah)	Northern kingdom (Israel)	Elijah, Elisha
Isaiah, Micah			Jonah
Nahum, Zephaniah,			Amos, Hosea

ASSYRIA

BABYLON

Nahum, Zephaniah, Jeremiah, Habakkuk, Ezekiel, Daniel, Haggai, Zechariah, Malachi

Ezra, Nehemiah

Jesus

heart towards other gods, and he began to oppress the people (1 Kings 11).

The decline into exile and the rise of prophecy

When Solomon's son, Rehoboam, succeeded him, the people asked for relief from their oppression (1 Kings 12). Rehoboam's older counsellors advised a conciliatory approach, but Rehoboam ignored them in favour of his peers, who told him to threaten the people with harsher treatment. The result was rebellion and in 931 BC the kingdom was divided. The ten northern tribes, who were known as Israel while the kingdom was divided, chose a new king—Jeroboam. The two southern tribes continued to follow Rehoboam and were known as Judah. The two nations lived in intermittent conflict (1 and 2 Kings).

In the northern kingdom there was a series of coups, culminating in the ascendancy of King Ahab to the throne. Ahab, influenced by his foreign wife, Jezebel, promoted the religion of the false god Baal (1 Kings 16). God sent Elijah and Elisha to call the people of the northern kingdom back to God. Elijah challenged the prophets of Baal to a contest on Mount Carmel (1 Kings 18). Altars were built and sacrifices were prepared. Elijah invited the prophets of Baal to prove the power of Baal by calling on him to provide fire. The prophets of Baal called on their god all day, but no fire came. When Elijah prayed, God answered immediately with fire that not only consumed the sacrifice, but the stones of the altar. Yet despite the ministry of the prophets, the people would not follow God. In 722 BC the northern kingdom was defeated by the Assyrians, exiled, and lost from history (2 Kings 17).

Meanwhile in the southern kingdom God was faithful to His promise to David. The throne passed down through

David's family. When the Assyrians attacked Jerusalem, King Hezekiah prayed to God for deliverance, and God defeated the Assyrian army (2 Kings 18 – 19 and Isaiah 36 – 37). But most of the kings were not faithful to God and turned the hearts of the people from Him. The nation's decline reached a climax with King Manasseh (2 Kings 21). During his reign the people did not just follow the ways of the nations, but "they did more evil than the nations the LORD had destroyed before the Israelites" (2 Kings 21 v 9).

King Josiah led a movement of reform, but it was too late. He could not deliver the people or turn back God's judgment (2 Kings 22 – 23). Eventually the nation was defeated by the Babylonians, who took the elite of Jerusalem back to Babylon (2 Kings 24). These included a young man called Daniel, whose ability to interpret dreams soon made him a valued member of the Babylonian court (Daniel 2 and 4). In this context Daniel remained faithful to the God of Israel. Courtiers jealous of Daniel's success persuaded the king of Babylon to decree that prayers should only be offered to himself (Daniel 6). Daniel, however, continued to pray to God. His punishment was to be thrown into a den of lions, but God sent an angel who closed their mouths.

Another of the early exiles was a trainee priest called Ezekiel, called by God to be a prophet (Ezekiel 1 – 3). His message was that hopes for national renewal were misplaced (Ezekiel 4 – 24). God would judge His people. His ministry overlapped that of Jeremiah, who spoke a similar message to those back in Jerusalem. But Ezekiel and Jeremiah were not heeded. The people of Jerusalem rebelled unsuccessfully against Babylon. In 587 BC the city was defeated, the temple destroyed and the people exiled (2 Kings 25). It was in Babylon that the Israelites were first called Jews.

Ezekiel, Jeremiah and the other prophets also spoke

words of hope. The promise of God still stood and God was faithful. Isaiah looked forward to a day when God would re-establish His kingdom through a new King David (Isaiah 9 and 11). Ezekiel saw that God would send the promised Saviour to rescue and renew His people (Ezekiel 34 – 37). Jeremiah spoke of a new covenant that God would make with His people, in which their sins would be forgiven and they would know God personally (Jeremiah 31 v 31-34).

Jeremiah also said that after 70 years the people would return to Jerusalem (Jeremiah 25 v 12). And so it was. The Babylonians were defeated by the Persians (Daniel 5) and the Persians allowed a group of Jews to return to Jerusalem under the leadership of Ezra (Ezra 1 – 2). The temple was rebuilt, though it was a pale shadow of Solomon's temple (Ezra 3; Haggai 2). But things did not go well. When a Jewish official called Nehemiah in the court of the Persians heard how bad things were he got permission to return to Jerusalem. Nehemiah succeeded in rebuilding the walls of Jerusalem (Nehemiah 1 – 6) but he could not reform the people or give them rest from their enemies (Nehemiah 7 – 13). In one sense the exile was over, but the kingdom of God had not been re-established.

Figure 12: Jesus

Ezra, Nehemiah

Jesus

Pentecost
Paul

Jesus

As God revealed to Daniel (Daniel 11), Persian rule became Greek rule. There was a period when the Jews regained autonomy under the leadership of Judas Maccabaeus. But then they, like most of the Mediterranean world, came under the authority of the Romans. Throughout this time—some 400 years—there was no word from God.

Then the silence was broken. An angel came to a young girl called Mary to tell her that she would bear a son. Mary was engaged to be married to Joseph, but she was still a virgin. Her child would be called Jesus, which means "saviour" (Luke 1). The angels who appeared to Mary, Joseph and those who witnessed the child's birth made it clear that this child was the promised Saviour and the King who would reign on David's throne (Matthew 1; Luke 1). This child was going to be the one promised to Adam and Eve, who would defeat the work of Satan (Genesis 3 v 15). Throughout the Old Testament story we have been asking: Who is the one offspring through whom the blessing of salvation will come? Now the promised one was here (Galatians 3 v 16). Indeed, the child was described as "Immanuel", which means "God with us" (Matthew 1 v 23). The promised Saviour was none other than God Himself taking on human flesh (John 1 v 14, 18). God Himself was coming to His people to set them free.

At around the age of 30 Jesus began His public ministry. Through miraculous signs He demonstrated His authority over sickness, evil spirits, the natural world and even death (Mark 1; 4 – 5). He claimed the authority to forgive sin and demonstrated the grace of God as He welcomed sinners (Mark 2; Luke 7). He was God's King come to re-establish God's kingdom. He was rejected by the Jewish leaders and so He chose twelve followers to constitute a new Israel—a new people of God (Mark 3). Much of His ministry was conducted in the northern part of Palestine, but there came a point when He headed towards Jerusalem, knowing that there He would meet His death (Luke 9 v 51). As they walked towards Jerusalem, Jesus spoke to His followers about His coming death and said His own sacrifice and service was a model of what it meant to follow Him. The crowds acclaimed Him as He entered Jerusalem (Mark 11), but in Jerusalem His conflict with the Jewish leaders reached its climax (Mark 11 – 13). One of His followers betrayed Him and Jesus was condemned to death, first by the Jews and then before the Roman Governor, Pilate (Mark 14 – 15). He was executed by being nailed to a cross of wood. As He died, darkness came over the land. He died forsaken by God, bearing the judgment of His people in their place. At the very end He cried out: "It is finished" (John 19 v 30). The work of salvation was not completed at the head of an army, or through a mighty miracle, but on a cross. The underlying problems of sin and death were dealt with through a substitute. Jesus died in our place (2 Corinthians 5 v 21).

On the third day after His death a group of women went to Jesus' tomb to anoint His body (Mark 16). They found the entrance stone rolled away and the tomb empty. Angels appeared to them, telling them not to look for the living among the dead (Luke 24 v 5). Jesus had risen. Death had been defeated. The promise of new life and a new creation had been confirmed.

The risen Jesus appeared to His disciples. He commissioned them to take the good news of salvation to all nations (Matthew 28; Luke 24). He promised to send the Spirit of God to help them fulfil this task (Acts 1 v 8). Finally He ascended into heaven with the promise that one day He would return in glory (Acts 1 v 9-11).

Figure 13: The church

The church

Forty days later, as the followers of Jesus gathered in Jerusalem, the Spirit of God came upon them as Jesus had promised (Acts 2). Something like a great wind ripped through the building and what seemed to be tongues of fire came to rest on the disciples. As the first Christians praised God, people heard them speak in many different languages. They declared that Jesus was Lord; that the one who had been crucified had been raised by God from the dead. Three thousand people responded to their call to believe in Jesus and be baptised.

The Christian community in Jerusalem was persecuted by the authorities (Acts 4 – 7). Many of its members were scattered, but as they went they took the good news of salvation with them, and Christian communities were formed in other areas (Acts 8 v 1-4). One of the leaders of the persecution was a man named Saul. One day, as he travelled to Damascus to arrest Christians, he saw a vision of the risen Jesus. Saul, who became known as Paul, became a follower of Jesus and a powerful missionary, taking the good news of salvation to Jews and Gentiles (non-Jews) across the Roman world.

Paul realised that the coming of Jesus marked the beginning of a new age—an age of grace and life in which God reigned (Romans 5). The old age of sin and death continued, but with the resurrection of Jesus and the coming of the Spirit the new age had begun. When Christ returns, the old age will finish and the new age will be consummated. In the meantime there is tension between the two ages.

Figure 14: The old age and the new age

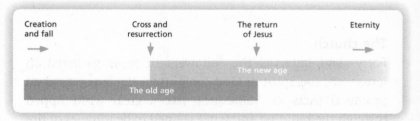

Figure 15: The old life and the new life

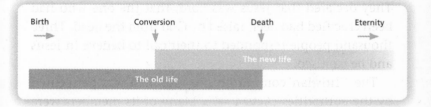

Christians experience this tension in their own lives. We are born as members of the old age, but when we trust in Jesus we become part of the new age. We experience new life through the Spirit of God, but still struggle with sin and death (Romans 6 – 8). The Spirit is the foretaste of the new age. The Spirit brings the new age, as it were, into the present experience of the Christian community.

The church grew and continued to grow over the following centuries. It has endured many times of persecution. It has also suffered times of complacency when it has lost its grasp of the truth. But still today it grows and spreads throughout the world.

This is the point in the story in which we are located. This story is our story. The story of Abraham, Moses, David and Jesus is our story. This story should provide our world-view, our values and our hope. We should consciously make this story our own. It should shape who we are even more than our family origins or national histories. We have roots that stretch back to the promise of Abraham and we have a future hope that stretches into eternity.

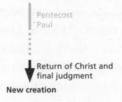

Figure 16: New creation

New creation

Jesus promised that one day He would return to earth. At His first coming He began to re-establish the rule of God. But the Bible looks forward to the day when the glory of God will once again fill the earth as the waters cover the sea (Habakkuk 2 v 14). Jesus will return to judge all people—living and dead (Matthew 25; Acts 17 v 31). There will be a great day of judgment when those who have rejected Jesus will be condemned to eternal judgment. But those who look to Jesus for salvation will receive eternal life in the presence of God.

Figure 17: The overlap of the ages

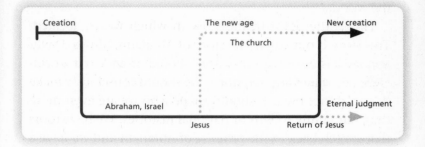

Late in his life John, one of Jesus' first followers, was exiled to an island called Patmos (Revelation 1 v 9-11). There he saw a vision of the new creation that God promises (Revelation 21 – 22). Heaven and earth will be united. God will dwell with His people. God will wipe away every tear and death will be no more. As C. S. Lewis suggests at the conclusion of his *Narnia Chronicles*, the end of the story is really the beginning of a much greater story that goes on for all eternity, and in which each chapter is better than the previous one.

Chapter 2

The promise of a people who know God

Figure 18: The promise of a people who know God: Outline

Creation	Humanity with God
Fall	Humanity alienated
Abraham	A people promised
Israel	A people set free *The promise of God is not fully fulfilled* *The people of God are not fully faithful*
Into exile	A people in captivity
Prophecy	A new people, a remnant people
Jesus	*The promise of God is fully fulfilled* *–Jesus is God with us* *The people of God are fully faithful* *–Jesus is God's faithful remnant*
The church	A new people
New creation	A new humanity

Creation: Humanity with God

Have you ever wondered why God created humanity? In the account of creation in Genesis 1 we read:

> **Genesis 1 v 26-27**
> Then God said, "Let us make man in our image, in our likeness, and let them rule over the fish of the sea and the birds of the air, over the livestock, over all the earth, and over all the creatures that move along the ground."
> So God created man
> in his own image,
> in the image of God
> he created him;
> male and female
> he created them.

The plural pronoun, "Let *us* make man", suggests God is **plural** and **communal**. God creates through His word and now that word is addressed to Himself. God is personal and He exists in community. What constitutes the image of God in man is a much-debated issue, but it seems that one element of what it means to be God's image-bearers is this communal nature. The God who said: "Let *us*" makes us relational beings. We are people in community. He did not make us solitary. We are made male and female. We are made to exist in community and we are made for community with God. The trinitarian community graciously extends its communal life.

We are not made of necessity. God did not make us because He needed us. He did not make us to complete a lack within Himself. Creation is an act of grace. God had no need of humanity. He had no need of a relationship outside the perfect relationships of the Trinity. Yet in an act of sheer grace He created us to share the life of the Trinity. To summarise:

• We were made for community (a people)
• We were made to know God (a people who know God)

God's purpose in creation was to have a people who know God.

Fall: Humanity alienated from God and one another

Genesis 3 v 6-10

When the woman saw that the fruit of the tree was good for food and pleasing to the eye, and also desirable for gaining wisdom, she took some and ate it. She also gave some to her husband, who was with her, and he ate it. Then the eyes of both of them were opened, and they realised that they were naked; so they sewed fig leaves together and made coverings for themselves.

Then the man and his wife heard the sound of the Lord God as he was walking in the garden in the cool of the day, and they hid from the Lord God among the trees of the garden. But the Lord God called to the man, "Where are you?"

He answered, "I heard you in the garden, and I was afraid because I was naked; so I hid."

We were made to know God. But after the fall Adam and Eve hide themselves from God. They can no longer walk with God in the garden. They are expelled from His presence. There is enmity between God and humanity. God has become our enemy.

We were also made for community. But now Adam and Eve hide themselves from one another—they cover their nakedness. There is enmity between the man and the woman. In Genesis 4 we again see conflict between people as Cain kills his brother Abel.

But there is hope. "And I will put enmity between you and the woman, and between your offspring and hers; he will crush your head, and you will strike his heel" (Genesis 3 v 15). Genesis 5 is a list of names. It is described as the "account of Adam's line" (Genesis 5 v 1). It appears somewhat boring to us, but it matters, because from the descendants of Adam will come someone who will defeat Satan and restore what Satan has destroyed.

Abraham: a people promised

Genesis 15 v 1-6

After this, the word of the LORD came to Abram in a vision:

"Do not be afraid, Abram. I am your shield, your very great reward."

But Abram said, "O Sovereign LORD, what can you give me since I remain childless and the one who will inherit my estate is Eliezer of Damascus?" And Abram said, "You have given me no children; so a servant in my household will be my heir."

Then the word of the LORD came to him: "This man will not be your heir, but a son coming from your own body will be your heir." He took him outside and said, "Look up at the heavens and count the stars—if indeed you can count them." Then he said to him, "So shall your offspring be."

Abram believed the LORD, and he credited it to him as
righteousness.

God promises to bless all nations through Abraham's
offspring. It is an amazing thing to have said to you.
But there is a problem. Abraham and his wife, Sarah, are
childless. Sarah is barren and they are both past the age of
childbearing.

It is like a tragic joke. God decides to bless all nations
through the descendants of one person. But then He
chooses an elderly, infertile couple. It certainly causes
Abraham and Sarah some amusement. The book of Genesis
says "Abraham fell face down; he laughed"—he "fell about
laughing", we might say.

Genesis 17 v 17-18
Abraham fell face down; he laughed and said to himself,
"Will a son be born to a man a hundred years old? Will Sarah
bear a child at the age of ninety?" And Abraham said to God,
"If only Ishmael might live under your blessing!"

The reference to Ishmael is important. Ishmael had been
born because Abraham and Sarah did not believe the
promise of God to them. God had promised a child, and
they had decided to take matters into their own hands.
Sarah, following a practice of the culture of the day, gave
Abraham her maidservant, Hagar. The key issue is not the
immorality of this action, but its faithlessness. Abraham
and Sarah do not trust the word of God. Still God graciously
reaffirms His promise in Genesis 17 v 19-22.

In Genesis 18 it is Sarah's turn to laugh.

Genesis 18 v 10-15

Then the LORD said, "I will surely return to you about this time next year, and Sarah your wife will have a son."

Now Sarah was listening at the entrance to the tent, which was behind him. Abraham and Sarah were already old and well advanced in years, and Sarah was past the age of childbearing. So Sarah laughed to herself as she thought, "After I am worn out and my master is old, will I now have this pleasure?"

Then the LORD said to Abraham, "Why did Sarah laugh and say, 'Will I really have a child, now that I am old?' Is anything too hard for the LORD? I will return to you at the appointed time next year and Sarah will have a son."

Sarah was afraid, so she lied and said, "I did not laugh." But he said, "Yes, you did laugh."

God promises the world to Abraham's descendants, but Abraham will have no descendants because Sarah is old and barren. What a joke! But here is the punchline. Sarah does conceive and has a child called Isaac (Genesis 21 v 1-7). The name "Isaac" means "laughter". God has the last laugh. The promise brought laughter to Sarah. She laughed when she heard it because it seemed a joke. Now she laughs again—this time with joy rather than derision—when the promise is fulfilled. It is the same story with the next generation (Genesis 25 v 21) and the next (Genesis 30 v 1-2, 22-24). God continues the line of promise despite barren women.

What is the point of all this? Why does God choose a family that repeatedly experiences infertility? God is demonstrating that the promise of salvation will be achieved by His power and His grace. Abraham and Sarah are impotent, quite literally. They cannot achieve God's purposes. When they try to do so, they create a horrible mess. Sarah is jealous and Hagar is sent away. In Genesis 21 v 1 we read: "Now the LORD was gracious to Sarah as he had said, and the LORD did for Sarah what he had promised." God was gracious. This is going to be a central theme of the Bible story—the story of promise. God achieves His purposes not on the back of human achievement but through His grace.

When Sarah laughs at the promise of God, God responds with a question: "Is anything too hard for the LORD?" (Genesis 18 v 14). In one sense Isaac is the answer to that question. But it finds an echo in Luke 1 v 34-37. The angel tells Mary she will have a child. Mary asks: "How this can be?", since she is a virgin. And the angel says: "Nothing is impossible with God" (Luke 1 v 37). In Luke 1 another child is promised to a barren elderly woman—John the Baptist to Elizabeth. But if an elderly, barren woman is a sign of God's grace and power, how much more the birth of a child to a virgin. The virgin birth is the culmination of a pattern (compare 1 Samuel 2 v 1-10 and Luke 1 v 46-55). God is making it clear that His purposes are achieved through His grace and power.

A people who know God

The promise to Abraham is not just of a people, but a people who know God. The presence of God is with Abraham, Isaac and Jacob (Genesis 21 v 22; 26 v 24, 28-29; 28 v 15). They can be a people who know God because they receive righteousness through faith. The blessing is not just to be a people, but to be a justified people—a people who are right with God. The fall into sin led to humanity's alienation and separation from God. But the relationship with God is restored through faith in the promise. Paul, citing Genesis 15 v 6, says that Abraham was "justified" because his faith in the promise of God was credited to him as righteousness. He looked to the fulfilment of the promise in the redemptive work of Jesus, just as we look back to that redemptive work:

Romans 4 v 1-3, 23-25

What then shall we say that Abraham, our forefather, discovered in this matter? If, in fact, Abraham was justified by works, he had something to boast about—but not before God. What does the Scripture say? "Abraham believed God, and it was credited to him as righteousness."

The words "it was credited to him" were written not for him alone, but also for us, to whom God will credit righteousness—for us who believe in him who raised Jesus our Lord from the dead. He was delivered over to death for our sins and was raised to life for our justification.

The New Testament presents Abraham as a model of how we should respond to the grace and promises of God:

Hebrews 11 v 11-12

By faith Abraham, even though he was past age—and Sarah herself was barren—was enabled to become a father because he considered him faithful who had made the promise. And so from this one man, and he as good as dead, came descendants as numerous as the stars in the sky and as countless as the sand on the seashore.

In Genesis 42 v 1-2 there is a new threat to the people of promise: famine. But God has already been at work. Through extraordinary providence, God has arranged things so that one of the family of promise—Joseph—is second-in-command in Egypt, the greatest power of the day. Joseph brings his family to Egypt, where they are safe from famine and where they prosper.

Israel: a people set free

When we come to the opening chapter of Exodus, we find that the promise of a people has been fulfilled: "The Israelites were fruitful and multiplied greatly and became exceedingly numerous, so that the land was filled with them" (Exodus 1 v 7). The family has become a nation. But they are a people who are enslaved. Their strength has caused the Egyptians to fear them and Pharaoh has conscripted them. They are not free and, in particular, they are not free to worship God. God's purpose was not only to create a people, but also a people who would know Him.

Exodus 3 v 7-15

The Lord said, "I have indeed seen the misery of my people in Egypt. I have heard them crying out because of their slave drivers, and I am concerned about their suffering. So I have come down to rescue them from the hand of the Egyptians and to bring them up out of that land into a good and spacious land, a land flowing with milk and honey—the home of the Canaanites, Hittites, Amorites, Perizzites, Hivites and Jebusites. And now the cry of the Israelites has reached me, and I have seen the way the Egyptians are oppressing them. So now, go. I am sending you to Pharaoh to bring my people the Israelites out of Egypt."

But Moses said to God, "Who am I, that I should go to Pharaoh and bring the Israelites out of Egypt?"

And God said, "I will be with you. And this will be the sign to you that it is I who have sent you: When you have brought the people out of Egypt, you will worship God on this mountain."

Moses said to God, "Suppose I go to the Israelites and say to them, 'The God of your fathers has sent me to you,' and they ask me, 'What is his name?' Then what shall I tell them?"

God said to Moses, "I AM WHO I AM. This is what you are to say to the Israelites: 'I AM has sent me to you.'"

God also said to Moses, "Say to the Israelites, 'The LORD, the God of your fathers—the God of Abraham, the God of Isaac and the God of Jacob—has sent me to you.' This is my name for ever, the name by which I am to be remembered from generation to generation."

God says that He has seen the misery of "my people". Not only that, but He has "come down" (3 v 7-8). God has come down to be with His people and He will set them free to worship Him (3 v 12).

God also gives to Moses a new revelation of His name. In the Bible a person's name often represents their character. God is the eternal I AM. It is from this we get the name Yahweh (Jehovah), the LORD. Yahweh, the LORD, is the covenant God of Israel. And the covenant LORD will act to keep His promise to Abraham (see also Exodus 2 v 23-25). The new revelation took place not simply at the bush, but in the whole redemption from Egypt. Forever after the LORD would be known as the exodus God, who had redeemed His people in faithfulness to His promise. He was the God like no other god—faithful, liberating and sovereign.

Moses goes with this message to the Pharaoh. But Pharaoh responds by making things worse for the Israelites. Now they must collect their own straw to make bricks, without any reduction in the quota. The people complain to Moses and Moses complains to God: "O Lord, why have you brought trouble upon this people?" (Exodus 5 v 22).

Exodus 6 v 2-8
God also said to Moses, "I am the LORD. I appeared to Abraham, to Isaac and to Jacob as God Almighty, but by my name the LORD I did not make myself known to them. I also established my covenant with them to give them the land of Canaan, where they lived as aliens. Moreover, I have heard the groaning of the Israelites, whom the Egyptians are enslaving, and I have remembered my covenant.

"Therefore, say to the Israelites: 'I am the LORD, and I will bring you out from under the yoke of the Egyptians. I will free you from being slaves to them, and I will redeem you with an outstretched arm and with mighty acts of judgment. I will take you as my own people, and I will be your God. Then you will know that I am the LORD your God, who brought you out from under the yoke of the Egyptians. And I will bring you to the land I swore with uplifted hand to give to Abraham, to Isaac and to Jacob. I will give it to you as a possession. I am the LORD.'"

Here again we see the same themes:
- God will act because of His promise to Abraham
- God Himself will set the people free—notice the repetition of "I will..."
- God will set them free in order to know Him.

- God has given Moses a new revelation of His name—He is the LORD, the covenant God of Israel.

What is driving the story on is the promise of God to Abraham (Exodus 2 v 23-25; 3 v 15; 6 v 3). The story of the Bible is the story of God "remembering" His promise to Abraham and acting to keep it. When God is said to remember His covenant, it does not mean He had previously forgotten it. It means He is acting in accordance with His covenant promises.

At the heart of God's purposes in the exodus from Egypt is the promise "I will take you as my own people, and I will be your God" (6 v 7). They are not only redeemed *from* slavery; they are also redeemed *to* know God. This promise that "I will be their God and they will my people" runs throughout the biblical narrative, forming one of its central themes.

Through the exodus God fulfils the first element of His promise to Abraham. Abraham's descendants become a nation free to worship God. God is with them to protect and guide them. The blessing of the priests captures the gracious presence of God beautifully when it pronounces: "The LORD bless you and keep you; the LORD make his face shine upon you" (Numbers 6 v 22-27). God "moves" with His people through the desert as the tabernacle is transported and erected with the people. In time, once the people have settled in the land, the temple is built and becomes the great symbol of God's presence with His people.

But this is not the end of the story. What God does through the exodus does not complete His purposes.

1. Israel points forward because the promise of God is not fully fulfilled

At Mount Sinai the people meet with God. Or rather, they almost meet God, for rescue from Egypt is only a picture of the redemption that God intends for His people, a redemption from the root problems of sin and death. When they encounter God at Sinai, it is a long way from the experience of Adam and Eve walking in the garden. They must ritually purify themselves, reminding them that their sin cuts them off from God. Limits are placed around the mountain because those who step onto the mountain or press forward to see the LORD will die—the LORD "will break out against them" (Exodus 19 v 12, 21, 24). As the firestorm of God's presence covers the mountain, we read: "Everyone in the camp trembled" (Exodus 19 v 16). God is present with His people, but it is hardly the intimate relationship for which we were made.

2. Israel points forward because the people of God are not fully faithful

God has set His people free that they might know Him and worship Him. They have just witnessed His splendour coming down on the mountain. Yet while Moses is receiving the law from God, they turn from worshipping God to worship a golden calf (Exodus 32). This sets the pattern of Israel's faithlessness and idolatry. Israel's history is plagued by idolatry. Idolatry is serving something other than the God we were made to know and whom Israel was set free to worship. As a result, from now on Israel's knowledge of God is mediated.

Figure 19: Exodus 32 – 33: God's people need a mediator

Exodus 32 v 30-35	Moses intercedes on behalf of the people.
Exodus 33 v 1-6	God will go before His people, but He will not be near them.
Exodus 33 v 7-11	The people will know God through a mediator, Moses. Only Moses speaks to God "as a man speaks with his friend".
Exodus 33 v 12-17	Without God's presence the people have no future. Moses reminds God that they are "your people".
Exodus 33 v 18-23	Even Moses can only see the afterglow of the rear part of God's glory.

How can a holy God live among sinful people? The book of Leviticus provides two responses:

1. Atonement through sacrifice and the mediation of a priest (Leviticus 1 – 10; 16)
2. Ritual and moral holiness (Leviticus 11 – 25)

Leviticus 15 v 31
"You must keep the Israelites separate from things that make them unclean, so they will not die in their uncleanness for defiling my dwelling-place, which is among them."

But the book of Leviticus is not so much a solution as a statement of the questions. Which sacrifice will deal with sin completely? After all, a dead sheep is not going to satisfy an infinitely holy God. Which priest will mediate forever? How can we be made holy internally as well as externally? How can the root problem of our sinful hearts be dealt with? For the answer we must turn to the reflections of the writer of Hebrews on the work of Christ.

Hebrews 10 v 10-14

And by that will, we have been made holy through the sacrifice of the body of Jesus Christ once for all.

Day after day every priest stands and performs his religious duties; again and again he offers the same sacrifices, which can never take away sins. But when this priest had offered for all time one sacrifice for sins, he sat down at the right hand of God. Since that time he waits for his enemies to be made his footstool, because by one sacrifice he has made perfect for ever those who are being made holy.

Notice that we cannot fully understand Leviticus until we understand Christ. But also, we cannot fully understand Christ until we have had a good look at Leviticus.

Decline into exile: a people in captivity

In 1 Kings 4 v 20 the writer says: "The people of Judah and Israel were as numerous as the sand on the seashore; they ate, they drank and they were happy." This is the language of the promise of Isaac and Jacob (Genesis 22 v 17; 32 v 12). But this high point in the fulfilment of the promise is short lived. In 1 Kings 12 the nation of Israel is divided. Solomon's son, Rehoboam, oppresses the people until Jeroboam leads a revolt. The nation divides with the ten northern tribes, usually known as Israel, led by Jeroboam and the two southern tribes, usually known as Judah, led by Rehoboam. Jeroboam sets up golden calves (12 v 25-33). He comes from Egypt to rescue the people from slavery. He sounds like a new Moses. But he turns out to be a new Aaron.

Exodus 32 v 4

[Aaron] took what they handed him and made it into an idol

cast in the shape of a calf, fashioning it with a tool. Then
they said, "These are your gods, O Israel, who brought you
up out of Egypt."

1 Kings 12 v 28
After seeking advice, the king made two golden calves.
He said to the people, "It is too much for you to go up to
Jerusalem. Here are your gods, O Israel, who brought you up
out of Egypt."

The people created by God to worship God have become
a divided people, worshipping idols. As a result Jeroboam
becomes in the mind of the writer of Kings the epitome of
an evil king who leads the people astray.

The faithlessness begun in Exodus 32 with the first golden
calf, and echoed in the golden calves of Jeroboam, continues
with only a few remissions until God comes in judgment.
These are a people who will not know God. They refuse
God's offer of friendship. They will not be His people. First
the northern kingdom is exiled and lost. Then the southern
kingdom is defeated by Babylon and goes into captivity.
Nebuchadnezzar defeats Judah and takes the people into
exile in Babylon (2 Kings 24 v 10-14; 25 v 11).

There is a poignant postscript. The few people left in
Judah assassinated Babylon's puppet king: "At this, all the
people from the least to the greatest, together with the army
officers, fled to Egypt for fear of the Babylonians" (2 Kings
25 v 26). After all these years of freedom and nationhood,
we are back in Egypt.

Prophecy: a remnant people

A new people

Jeremiah 31 v 31-34

"The time is coming," declares the LORD, "when I will make a new covenant with the house of Israel and with the house of Judah. It will not be like the covenant I made with their forefathers when I took them by the hand to lead them out of Egypt, because they broke my covenant, though I was a husband to them," declares the LORD. "This is the covenant that I will make with the house of Israel after that time," declares the LORD. "I will put my law in their minds and write it on their hearts. I will be their God, and they will be my people. No longer will a man teach his neighbour, or a man his brother, saying, 'Know the LORD,' because they will all know me, from the least of them to the greatest," declares the LORD. "For I will forgive their wickedness and will remember their sins no more."

God will make a new covenant with His people because the nation of Israel broke the covenant. At the heart of this new covenant will be the fulfilment of the core promise: "I will be their God and they will be my people." People will no longer need a mediator. They will all know Him, from the least to the greatest, for God will deal with their sin once and for all.

A faithful remnant

As the prophets reflected on the unfaithfulness of God's people they were inspired to look for a remnant—a faithful few—that God would save.

Zechariah 13 v 7-9

"Awake, O sword, against my shepherd, against the man
who is close to me!" declares the LORD Almighty. "Strike the
shepherd, and the sheep will be scattered, and I will turn my
hand against the little ones." "In the whole land," declares
the LORD, "two-thirds will be struck down and perish; yet
one-third will be left in it. This third I will bring into the fire;
I will refine them like silver and test them like gold.

"They will call on my name and I will answer them; I will
say, 'They are my people,' and they will say, 'The LORD is our
God.'"

Zechariah says two-thirds of the people will perish but one-
third will be saved. They will call on God's name and be His
people.

Jesus: God with us and God's faithful people

1. In Jesus the promise of God is fully fulfilled
—He is God with us

Israel pointed forward because the promise of God was not
fully fulfilled in the experience of the nation. But in Jesus
the promise is fully fulfilled, for Jesus is God with us. He
makes God known. He is the way to the Father. In Him all
the fullness of the Deity dwells.

Matthew 1 v 23

"The virgin will be with child and will give birth to a son,
and they will call him 'Immanuel'—which means, 'God
with us.'"

John 1 v 18
No-one has ever seen God, but God the One and [the] Only
[Son], who is at the Father's side, has made him known.

Colossians 2 v 9-10
For in Christ all the fulness of the Deity lives in bodily form,
and you have been given fulness in Christ, who is the Head
over every power and authority.

2. In Jesus the people of God are fully faithful
—He is God's faithful remnant

Israel pointed forward because the people of God were not
fully faithful. Zechariah 13 v 7-9 spoke of a faithful remnant
made up of a third of the people. But the narrowing down
of the faithful to one-third of the people is not the end of
the story. Jesus Himself quotes these words on the night He
is arrested:

Matthew 26 v 31
"This very night you will all fall away on account of me, for
it is written: 'I will strike the shepherd, and the sheep of the
flock will be scattered.'"

Zechariah 13 ultimately points to a time when the faithful
remnant will come down to one person. On the night that
Jesus was betrayed, arrested, tried and sentenced to death,
He quoted these words about a remnant. When the enemies
of God move against the good shepherd, all the sheep are
scattered. Ultimately there is only one person who is faithful
to the end—the Lord Jesus Christ. At the moment of crisis
all His followers abandon Him.

This is reality. This is the human condition. We have all
abandoned God. None of us has been consistently faithful

to God. When we read the history of Israel's unfaithfulness we read our history. We see our own hearts.

But the faithfulness of Jesus to the very end—even to death—means those He represents are counted faithful. We can call on God's name and be His people. We can say "The LORD is our God" (Zechariah 13 v 9). Through Jesus' faithfulness we are counted faithful. Through trust in His name we become part of the faithful remnant. We become that immoveable rock that stands against God's enemies (Zechariah 12 v 3). We share in the salvation that God promises to His people.

Isaiah 5 v 1-7

I will sing for the one I love a song about his vineyard: My loved one had a vineyard on a fertile hillside. He dug it up and cleared it of stones and planted it with the choicest vines. He built a watchtower in it and cut out a winepress as well. Then he looked for a crop of good grapes, but it yielded only bad fruit.

"Now you dwellers in Jerusalem and men of Judah, judge between me and my vineyard. What more could have been done for my vineyard than I have done for it? When I looked for good grapes, why did it yield only bad? Now I will tell you what I am going to do to my vineyard: I will take away its hedge, and it will be destroyed; I will break down its wall, and it will be trampled. I will make it a wasteland, neither pruned nor cultivated, and briers and thorns will grow there. I will command the clouds not to rain on it."

The vineyard of the LORD Almighty is the house of Israel, and the men of Judah are the garden of his delight. And he looked for justice, but saw bloodshed; for righteousness, but heard cries of distress.

Isaiah describes the people as God's vineyard (see also Psalm 80 v 8-16; Isaiah 27 v 2-6; Jeremiah 2 v 21; 12 v 10-11; Ezekiel 15 v 1-8; 17 v 1-24; 19 v 10-14; Hosea 10 v 1-2). God has cared for it and protected it, but it has produced only bad fruit, and so it will be destroyed. Jeremiah says: "I had planted you like a choice vine of sound and reliable stock. How then did you turn against me into a corrupt, wild vine?" (Jeremiah 2 v 21). In John 15 v 1 Jesus says: "I am the true vine, and my Father is the gardener." He is echoing the language of the Old Testament. Israel was God's vine, but it produced bad fruit. Jesus is the true vine, who produces good fruit.

In Isaiah 49 v 1-7 God speaks of "my servant". The servant is variously described as the nation (Isaiah 49 v 3) and as an individual who will gather the nation to Himself (Isaiah 49 v 5-6). The servant is Israel and yet also distinct from Israel. The servant is the personification of the nation and yet also the saviour of the nation. How can this be? Jesus is the faithful "people" of God. He is the personification of the people of God as they should be and so, through His faithfulness, He saves a people for Himself. He gathers Israel to Himself and brings salvation to the ends of the earth (Isaiah 49 v 5-6).

The church: a new people
As God's faithful one, Jesus creates a new people who know God. The New Testament portrays Jesus as *both* God with us *and* God's faithful people. He represents both sides of the covenant. He is truly God and He is the truly faithful people of God. As a result He brings both parties together: "There

is ... one mediator between God and men, the man Christ Jesus" (1 Timothy 2 v 5). Jesus is creating a new people who know God.

2 Corinthians 6 v 14 – 7 v 1

Do not be yoked together with unbelievers. For what do righteousness and wickedness have in common? Or what fellowship can light have with darkness? What harmony is there between Christ and Belial? What does a believer have in common with an unbeliever? What agreement is there between the temple of God and idols? For we are the temple of the living God. As God has said: "I will live with them and walk among them, and I will be their God, and they will be my people."

"Therefore come out from them and be separate, says the LORD. Touch no unclean thing, and I will receive you." "I will be a Father to you, and you will be my sons and daughters, says the LORD Almighty." Since we have these promises, dear friends, let us purify ourselves from everything that contaminates body and spirit, perfecting holiness out of reverence for God.

Paul says that the promise that "I will live with them and walk among them, and I will be their God, and they will be my people" is fulfilled in the church. The church is the new Israel. It is in the church that God dwells with His people. And so we are to live as God's holy people. We are to live, as it were, as God's companions. It is of those in Christ that God now says: "I will be their God and they will be my people".

Figure 20 presents the story of the people of God in the form of a diagram. Abraham was chosen by God to be the

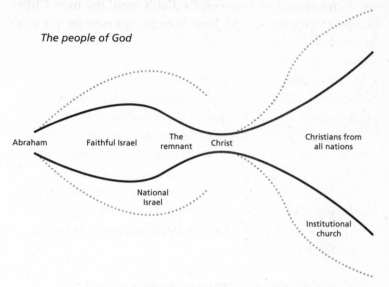

Figure 20: The story of the people of God

The people of God

Abraham   Faithful Israel   The remnant   Christ   Christians from all nations

National Israel

Institutional church

father of a new people—a people who would know God. He became the father of the nation of Israel. But not all within the nation of Israel shared Abraham's faith in the promise of God. National Israel was a wider group than faithful Israel. As Paul puts it: "Not all who are descended from Israel are Israel" (Romans 9 v 6). Gentiles could join the nation of Israel through the rite of circumcision, but it was by faith in the promise that they became part of the spiritual Israel—the true people of God. As the nation slipped into apostasy, the number of true believers dwindled until it was little more than a faithful remnant preserved by God. Finally that faithful remnant came down to one man—Jesus Christ. Jesus is the faithful one through whom all those who share the faith of Abraham are part of the true people of God. Through Him the blessing of membership of the people of God flows to all nations. Just as national Israel was wider in scope than the true spiritual Israel, so there are those within the institutional church who are not truly part of the people of God because they do not have true faith in Jesus. Christians are called Jews of the new covenant (Romans 2 v 28-29); the children of Abraham (Galatians 3 v 7); Abraham's seed (Galatians 3 v 29); the Israel of God (Galatians 6 v 16); citizens of Israel (Ephesians 2 v 19); the circumcision (Philippians 3 v 3); the twelve tribes (James 1 v 1); and a holy nation (1 Peter 2 v 9). In other words, the true people of God are no longer national Israel, but all those who have faith in Jesus Christ.

New creation: a new humanity

Revelation 21 v 1-4

Then I saw a new heaven and a new earth, for the first heaven and the first earth had passed away, and there was no longer any sea. I saw the Holy City, the new Jerusalem, coming down out of heaven from God, prepared as a bride beautifully dressed for her husband. And I heard a loud voice from the throne saying, "Now the dwelling of God is with men, and he will live with them. They will be his people, and God himself will be with them and be their God. He will wipe every tear from their eyes. There will be no more death or mourning or crying or pain, for the old order of things has passed away."

At the heart of the Apostle John's wonderful vision of the new creation is the fulfilment of the promise made through Moses: "They will be his people, and God himself will be with them and be their God" (21 v 3). And when God lives among you there is no death, mourning, crying or pain.

***

Case Study: The promise of a people and the book of Nehemiah

How does the theme of God's promise of a people who know Him help us understand the message of Nehemiah for Christians today?

The story of Nehemiah takes place shortly after the exile in Babylon. Babylon has been defeated by Persia and some Jews have returned to the promised land. Nehemiah is a Jew who has risen in the Persian civil service. One day his brother reports: "Those who survived the exile and are back in the province are in great trouble and disgrace. The wall of Jerusalem is broken down, and its gates have been burned with fire" (Nehemiah 1 v 3). The book is about how Nehemiah rebuilds the wall (chapters 2 – 7) and reforms the people (chapters 7 – 13).

Nehemiah 7 lists those who have returned from exile. The word of God is read to the people in Nehemiah 8. They respond with weeping and the prayer of confession in Nehemiah 9. Then in Nehemiah 10 they renew their commitment to God by making three vows. The people promise:

Figure 21: The three promises of Nehemiah 13

Not to intermarry	To keep the Sabbath	To maintain the temple
We promise not to give our daughters in marriage to the peoples around us or take their daughters for our sons. (10 v 30)	We will not buy from [the neighbouring peoples] on the Sabbath or on any holy day. (10 v 31)	We will not neglect the house of our God. (10 v 32-39)

But by Nehemiah 13 the people are:

Figure 22: The three broken promises of Nehemiah 13

Intermarrying	Breaking the Sabbath	Neglecting the temple
In those days I saw men of Judah who had married women from Ashdod, Ammon and Moab. (13 v 23-28)	Men from Tyre were ... selling ... in Jerusalem on the Sabbath to the people of Judah. (13 v 15-22)	So I rebuked the officials and asked them: "Why is the house of God neglected?" (13 v 6-13)

The three things they vowed before God to do are the very things of which they are now found guilty. The people have returned from exile. But they have not been set free from sin. So the prayer of Nehemiah 9 ends with the people needing a new exodus:

Nehemiah 9 v 36-37
"But see, we are slaves today, slaves in the land you gave our forefathers so that they could eat its fruit and the other good things it produces. Because of our sins, its abundant harvest goes to the kings you have placed over us. They rule over our bodies and our cattle as they please. We are in great distress."

Nehemiah's achievements are huge by any standards. He is faithful and courageous. He shows great integrity and kindness. But this is the point. Even the very best of men cannot renew the people or set them free. Nehemiah cannot deal with the underlying causes of the exile—the problem of sin and judgment. The book of Nehemiah highlights the need for God's Messiah.

Mark begins his Gospel with a quote from Isaiah 40 (Mark 1 v 3). It is the promise of one who will announce that the LORD is coming to end the exile and speak comfort to God's people (Isaiah 40 v 1-5). "And so John came" says Mark (1 v 4). John the Baptist announces the end of the exile because he announces the coming of the Christ. What Nehemiah could not achieve Jesus will accomplish—the liberation of God's people so that they can know God and be His people.

The promise of a place of blessing

Figure 23: The promise of a place of blessing: Outline

Creation	At home in Eden
Fall	Expelled from Eden
Abraham	A land promised
Israel	A land given, Jerusalem, temple: *Conquest did not fully fulfil the promise* *People were not fully faithful to the promise*
Into exile	A land lost
Prophecy	A land to be restored
Jesus	We find rest and blessing
The church	In Christ: *a salvation reality* *a communal reality* *a future reality*
New creation	A new creation

When we look at passages like Joshua 13 – 19 it is hard to know what to make of them. These lists of people and places seem of little value. We search through for a fragment of narrative. Yet Paul tells Timothy that "all Scripture is God-breathed and is useful for teaching, rebuking, correcting and training in righteousness" (2 Timothy 3 v 16). Presumably when Paul said "all" he included Joshua 13 – 19. How is Joshua 13 – 19 "useful" for us as Christians?

To us, an account of the geography of ancient Palestine seems boring, but the Israelites would have heard it read with eager interest. They were listening out for the name of their family. They were waiting for the confirmation that they had a plot in the land. They wanted to hear again about their share in the inheritance God had given His people. At one level, land was a central part of a largely agrarian economy. Your livelihood depended on your portion of land—land mattered in a way that it does not in the industrial economies of the contemporary west. But there was something much more fundamental going on. The land was part of the Israelites' identity and the provision of the land was integral to the saving acts that Yahweh had done among them.

Let us go back to the beginning and trace the theme of the land through the Bible story.

Creation: at home in Eden

God created humanity to be a people who will be His people. And He created the earth as a place of blessing for them to inhabit, to develop, and in which they could know Him to be a good God. Furthermore, He placed them in the Garden of Eden. God saw all that He made was good. Yet He made a specific place as a home for His people.

All the earth was good, but Eden was better. It was a place of blessing.

Genesis 2 v 8-9
Now the LORD God had planted a garden in the east, in Eden; and there he put the man he had formed. And the LORD God made all kinds of trees grow out of the ground—trees that were pleasing to the eye and good for food. In the middle of the garden were the tree of life and the tree of the knowledge of good and evil.

Eden is place of beauty ("pleasing to the eye") and provision ("good for food"). It is a place of security. The tree of life ensures in some way we are not told that humanity enjoys health and life. It is a place of communion with God—God walks with Adam and Eve.

Fall: expelled from Eden

But when humanity rejects God's good rule, they are expelled from Eden. Adam and Eve hide from God; they shun the presence of God. But the real problem of our sin is that God excludes us from His presence. We are cut off from Eden. We are cut off from the place of God's blessing. The angel with the flaming sword who prevents Adam and Eve returning to Eden becomes a symbol of humanity's separation from God (Genesis 3 v 23-24).

When Cain murders his brother, we read: "So Cain went out from the LORD's presence and lived in the land of Nod, east of Eden" (Genesis 4 v 16). In Genesis 3 v 24 Adam and Eve found themselves east of Eden. Now Cain is further east. In Genesis 11 v 2 humanity is still moving eastward—away from Eden—this time to the plain of Shinar, where the tower of Babel is erected in defiance of God. The geography of humanity's early movements highlights their distance from the place of God's blessing. In every sense we are a long way from walking with God in the garden.

Abraham: a land promised

Then God comes to Abraham and says: "Leave your country, your people and your father's household and go to the land I will show you" (Genesis 12 v 1). The story of Abraham begins with God calling him to leave his country and head out into the desert for a life in tents. He is called to a life of movement, pilgrimage and wandering in search of a land God has yet to show him. He is questing for the place of God's blessing to which God has called him.

The promise of God to Abraham is programmatic for the Bible story as a whole. It sets in train God's saving purposes. And one of the key components of that promise is the promise of a land:

Genesis 12 v 6-7
Abram travelled through the land as far as the site of the great tree of Moreh at Shechem. At that time the Canaanites were in the land. The LORD appeared to Abram and said, "To your offspring I will give this land."

Genesis 15 v 7
"I am the LORD, who brought you out of Ur of the Chaldeans to give you this land to take possession of it."

Genesis 17 v 8
"The whole land of Canaan, where you are now an alien, I will give as an everlasting possession to you and your descendants after you; and I will be their God."

God promises to give a land to Abraham and his descendants as "an everlasting possession". A time will come when the people of God will dwell in the place of God—the place of blessing—and they will dwell in it forever. God blesses Abraham's family in the land. In the midst of famine God tells Isaac he has no need to find food in Egypt because God will bless him in the land of promise (Genesis 26 v 1-6). "Isaac planted crops in that land and the same year reaped a hundredfold, because the LORD blessed him" (Genesis 26 v 12).

Israel: A land given with Jerusalem and the temple

By Exodus 1 the promise to Abraham of a people has become a reality. The one man has become a family and the family has become a nation. But in Exodus 1 they are in Egypt. They have left the land of promise. God's providential hand in Joseph's life by which He preserves the people of promise—and with them the future of the promise of salvation—has led to life in a foreign land. Jacob's last words are a request to be buried back in the land of promise (Genesis 49 v 29-33).

In Exodus 1 we discover that life outside the place of God is a life of slavery, threat and tyranny. The people have been enslaved by the Egyptians and the chapter ends with Pharaoh's decree that every male child is to be drowned in the Nile.

In Exodus 2 we read how one particular child is saved from being thrown in the Nile by being gently placed in a basket. The first readers of Exodus could not read this without knowing who this child was and what he would do. This was going to be Moses, brought up in the courts of Egypt, but destined to lead the Israelites to liberation and to receive the covenant from God on Sinai.

When Moses is forced to flee to Midian, he finds a welcome and a home. This is no coincidence, for Midian *is* home—it is part of the land of promise. The Midianites were nomads, but the area through which they roamed was Canaan. And here God is worshipped freely, in contrast to Egypt (Exodus 2 v 16; 3 v 6; 18 v 9-12). When Moses has a son, he calls him Gershom, and the correct translation of Moses' explanation of that name is "a stranger have I been in a land foreign to me" (2 v 22). In other words, it is a reference to Egypt, which, despite being the place of his birth and upbringing, Moses now sees as a foreign country. It is a great statement of faith in the promise of God. The promise of God to Abraham defines his identity more than his birth and upbringing. It is a statement every Christian should make about life in this world after his or her conversion. Now the land of birth and upbringing is a foreign land, for now we are pilgrims heading for the promised land, the home of heaven.

But this scene of domestic bliss and rest cannot be the end of the story.

Israel's liberator is tending sheep in Midian. Moses has found peace in the promised land. The narrative skilfully heightens the tension. Abraham's descendants have become a people, but they are far from the land of promise. Meanwhile Moses may have found peace in the land of promise, but he is apart from his people, the people of promise. In Exodus 1 we see the promise to Abraham fulfilled in a people—Israel becomes a nation. In Exodus 2 Moses finds the fulfilment of the second part—he finds a home in the promised land with the freedom to worship God. But there is terrible disjunction between these two elements.

Exodus 2 ends with God hearing the cry of the Israelites

in slavery and remembering His covenant with Abraham (2 v 23-25). God remembering the covenant in the Bible does not mean that He is forgetful. Instead it is the prelude to God acting to keep His promises. To remember is to act to fulfil what was promised.

The book of Exodus is the story of how God liberates His people and leads them through the Red Sea towards the land of promise. He remembers His covenant and so brings His people to the land of promise. He is faithful to His promises. But the people are not faithful to Him. They do not act in accordance with the promise. The majority of the spies sent into the land come back with tales of terrifying giants. We cannot take this land, they conclude, and the people agree. They do not trust the promise of God. They are not faithful. They do not act in accordance with the promise. If they had truly believed the promise they may have gulped at the giants, but they would have trusted God to fulfil what He had said. Instead they doubt and so they do not enter the land. They are destined to wander in the desert until another generation takes their place (Numbers 13 – 14).

Forty years on, God comes to Joshua, the new leader of Israel, and tells him that the time to take the land has come. Notice the language in which this call is made:

Joshua 1 v 1-9

"The land I am about to give ... I will give you every place where you set your foot, as I promised to Moses ... As I was with Moses, so I will be with you: I will never leave you or forsake you ... the land I swore to their forefathers to give them ... Have I not commanded it? ... the LORD you God will be with you..."

God will give the land to His people. It will be His gift. God will be with Joshua and the people. They must fight, but He will give them the victory. And God will give the land because of His promise to Abraham and to Moses.

And this is what God does. He preserves the spies through Rahab (Joshua 2). He parts the River Jordan (Joshua 3 – 4). He brings down the walls of Jericho in a way that made it unmistakeable that it was His hand (Joshua 6). He causes the sun to stand still while the five kings of the Amorites are defeated (Joshua 10). He gives Israel victory in two campaigns, one to the south (Joshua 10) and one to the north (Joshua 11). Things only go wrong when the people do not follow God—when they do not trust His word. Achan's sin leads to defeat by Ai (Joshua 7) and the hasty actions of the people lead to deception by the Gibeonites (Joshua 9; see Exodus 34 v 12,15).

In Joshua 5 v 13-15 Joshua has an encounter with a stranger. "Are you for us or for our enemies?" he asks (Joshua 5 v 13). The stranger replies: "Neither, but as commander of the army of the LORD I have now come" (Joshua 5 v 14). God is not at Israel's disposal. It is Israel who must obey God, not God who must do as they wish. But He has come and through His coming He graciously gives His people victory. The conclusion—indeed, the message—of the book of Joshua comes in Joshua 21:

Joshua 21 v 43-45
So the LORD gave Israel all the land he had sworn to give their forefathers, and they took possession of it and settled there. The LORD gave them rest on every side, just as he had sworn to their forefathers. Not one of their enemies withstood them; the LORD handed all their enemies over to

them. Not one of all the LORD's good promises to the house
of Israel failed; every one was fulfilled.

Notice again: Israel has taken possession of the land because
God has given it to her. And God has given the land to
Israel in fulfilment of His promise.

This emphasis on the land as a gift was anticipated in the
law of Moses. The gift of the land has ethical implications.
Just as a people liberated by the grace of God are to be a
liberating and gracious people, so a people who have
received the land as a gift are to be a generous people
(Leviticus 25 v 2,23-24).

But Joshua 21 is not the end of the story for two
reasons:

1. The people of the land were not fully faithful to God's
   promises—they accepted less than God intended.
2. The conquest of the land did not fully fulfil God's
   purposes—God intended more than the conquest of
   Canaan.

We will return to the second reason later. For now we will
explore the first reason: the people to whom God gave the
land were not faithful to Him. Joshua 21 does not present
the full story. It is true. God has been faithful. He has given
the people the land. But it is not the whole truth. Judges 1
presents another side to the picture. Here the people fail to
trust God's promise. They decide the enemy is too strong
and too well equipped (1 v 19). They are not faithful to the
promise and they compromise their identity as the distinct
people of promise (2 v 1-2).

Things start well enough (1 v 1-15). The tribe of Judah
conquers the land and destroys the inhabitants as God
commanded. In Judges 1 v 12-16 the writer records for us

the fulfilment of specific promises to Caleb (see Joshua 14 v 6-15) and the Kenites (see Numbers 10 v 29). In Judges 1 v 14-15 land is given simply because Acsah asks for it. This is intended as a model for Israel. If they trust in God, He will give them the land.

But the rest of the chapter is the story of increasing compromise. In verses 17-21 the Israelites fail to dislodge the Canaanites. In verses 22-26 they make treaties with the Canaanites, which God had forbidden them to do (see Exodus 34 v 12, 15). In verses 27-30 we find Canaanites living among Israelites, while in verses 31-33 it is the Israelites who live among Canaanites. Finally in verse 34 the narrative is about the actions of the Amorites: "The Amorites confined the Danites to the hill country, not allowing them to come down into the plain." The Israelite tribe of Dan are passive. They are not only failing to drive out the Canaanites, it is the Canaanites who are confining the Israelites.

This is not what God intended and so the angel of the LORD comes to pronounce judgment on the people. God will not drive out the remaining nations. Instead "they will be [thorns] in your sides" (Judges 2 v 3). The territory promised in Joshua 1 v 4 is not the territory held by the people of Israel. And the land is not a place of blessing. It is a place of threat.

Jerusalem

An important development takes place when King David captures Jerusalem and makes it his capital (2 Samuel 5 v 6-12). As Israel's hopes became focused in the dynasty of David, so the "place" of God became focused on the city of David—Jerusalem. Jerusalem and the mountain upon which it was built—Mount Zion—became the symbols of Israel's security and prosperity.

In Psalm 48 the psalmist describes Mount Zion as "beautiful in its loftiness, the joy of the whole earth" (48 v 2). Jerusalem is secure from the attack of her enemies (48 v 4-5). It is place of splendour (48 v 12-13). The reality, however, is that Mount Zion was not the loftiest mountain in the world and Jerusalem was not of great significance in the region. But the psalmist is reflecting a theological reality, not a political or geographic reality. What makes Jerusalem great is that God is with her: "God is in her citadels; he has shown himself to be her fortress ... God makes her secure for ever ... Mount Zion rejoices ... because of your judgments" (48 v 3,8,11). What makes Jerusalem special is that she is "the city of our God, his holy mountain" (48 v 1). Jerusalem is the place where God dwells. Psalm 48 is a great statement of Israelite faith. God has given the land to Israel with Jerusalem as its capital, and so her future is secure.

Decline into exile: the land lost, Jerusalem and the temple destroyed

God, Psalm 48 affirms, has given the land to Israel with Jerusalem as its capital and so her future is secure. But now read what happens when the Babylonians attack Jerusalem:

2 Chronicles 36 v 15-21

The LORD, the God of their fathers, sent word to them through his messengers again and again, because he had pity on his people and on his dwelling-place. But they mocked God's messengers, despised his words and scoffed at his prophets until the wrath of the LORD was aroused against his people and there was no remedy. He brought up against them the king of the Babylonians, who killed their young men with the sword in the sanctuary, and spared neither young man nor young woman, old man or aged. God handed all of them over to Nebuchadnezzar. He carried to Babylon all the articles from the temple of God, both large and small, and the treasures of the LORD's temple and the treasures of the king and his officials. They set fire to God's temple and broke down the wall of Jerusalem; they burned all the palaces and destroyed everything of value there.

He carried into exile to Babylon the remnant who escaped from the sword, and they became servants to him and his sons until the kingdom of Persia came to power. The land enjoyed its sabbath rests; all the time of its desolation it rested, until the seventy years were completed in fulfilment of the word of the LORD spoken by Jeremiah.

God gave his people the land as He promised—a land flowing with milk and honey, a place of security and rest. But now Jerusalem has fallen, its walls are destroyed, the temple pillaged, the land captured and the people exiled. Once again the people are away from the land of promise. This is obviously a political calamity, but it is also a theological calamity. The promise of God is in tatters. Is God unfaithful to His promise? Is He unable to keep what He promises? No, God is faithful and He is able. The reason for the exile lies elsewhere:

2 Chronicles 36 v 15-16
The LORD, the God of their fathers, sent word to them through his messengers again and again, because he had pity on his people and on his dwelling-place. But they mocked God's messengers, despised his words and scoffed at his prophets until the wrath of the LORD was aroused against his people and there was no remedy.

The problem is not that God has been unfaithful but that the people have been unfaithful. In one elusive reference the writer of Chronicles suggests something else: "The land enjoyed its sabbath rests; all the time of its desolation it rested, until the seventy years were completed in fulfilment of the word of the LORD spoken by Jeremiah" (2 Chronicles 36 v 21). The land was not only to be a place of rest from enemies—a rest Israel forfeited by her unfaithfulness. The land was also to be a place of what we might call "ecological rest". Every seventh year the land was to lie fallow—to enjoy a sabbath "rest". This was an expression of the people's trust in the provision of God. The God who had given the land would give prosperity in the land to those who continued to trust Him.

But now the writer of Chronicles suggests that one reason for the exile was because Israel had been unfaithful to this rest. The exile would allow the land to "catch up" on its sabbath rests. By some calculations Israel had lived in the land for 420 years. An exile of 70 years would mean that after 490 years the land would have enjoyed rest for one year in seven as God intended. If Israel would not live in the land as a land of gift and rest, then God would impose the sabbath rest through conquest and exile. This was just what the Levitical law warned would happen (Leviticus 26 v 32-35).

The theme of rest runs throughout the biblical narrative. On the seventh day of creation God began to rest. He made humanity to share that rest. The land of promise was to be a land of rest, where the people found prosperity and freedom from their enemies. But because of the people's unfaithfulness, the nations of Canaan remain as thorns in their sides (Judges 2 v 3). The land is not a place of peace. At his height David gave the people rest from their enemies

(2 Samuel 7 v 1), but it was short lived. Ultimately, God's people are overrun by their enemies and go into exile.

When the people return from exile under the leadership of Nehemiah, they are able to rebuild Jerusalem, but they do not enjoy rest from their enemies. For all his achievements, Nehemiah cannot provide rest in the promised land.

Prophecy: a Land to be restored with a New Jerusalem

Israel had focused on the gift and not on the Giver. They placed their hope in the strength of Jerusalem and not in God. The role of the prophets was in part to disabuse them of their false hopes. But as those hopes came crashing down—quite literally as the walls of Jerusalem fell—and as the promise of a land of blessing and security seemed to have come to nothing, the prophets also pointed to a restored land and a new Jerusalem.

Ezekiel 1 – 24 warns of coming judgment and explain the futility of Israel's false hopes. "God is against you," he tells the people. Chapters 25 – 32 are addressed to the nations, for Israel's fate will be their fate too, for God is against them as well. The pivot of the book comes in 33 v 21-22, when a man comes to Ezekiel to tell him the long-awaited news that Jerusalem has fallen. With this news Ezekiel's "mouth was opened" and he is able to speak words of hope. One theme of that hope is that God will restore His people to a restored land:

Ezekiel 36 v 33-34

This is what the Sovereign LORD says: "On the day I cleanse you from all your sins, I will resettle your towns, and the ruins will be rebuilt. The desolate land will be cultivated instead of lying desolate in the sight of all who pass through it."

The prophecy of Ezekiel ends with a vision of a new temple in a new Jerusalem. The final chapter describes the dimensions of the new city and the book ends with the name of the city: "The Lord is there" (48 v 35).

But Ezekiel speaks of more than a restored land for he speaks of its restoration in terms of a new Eden: "They will say, 'This land that was laid waste has become like the garden of Eden'" (36 v 35). Ezekiel sees a river flowing from the new temple that makes salt water fresh. By the banks of this life-giving river are trees that bear fruit each month and whose leaves bring healing (47 v 1-12). We are back in Eden. We are back with the tree of life.

Jesus: The one in whom we find rest and blessing

Where is the place where we can find God's blessing? Where on earth can we find rest and peace? Not in Palestine, for sadly that has remained a place of conflict. A number of societies thought they could build the place of God on earth by establishing a godly society. But none lasted long. But there is a place where we can find blessing, rest and peace. That place is in Christ.

God promises a land of blessing and rest to His people. Joshua, David and Nehemiah partially fulfilled this promise, but what they achieved fell far short of what God intended. The prophets spoke of a coming day when God would restore His people to a restored land. They spoke of rest in a new Eden.

This is the context in which Jesus said: "Come to me, all you who are weary and burdened, and I will give you rest" (Matthew 11 v 28). This is not an existential statement of individual piety. It is an "exodus" statement. It is the promise of liberation—liberation from the enemies of sin, religious law and death, and liberation into a place of blessing and rest. Jesus offers what Joshua—his namesake ("Joshua" is the Hebrew form of "Jesus")—could not achieve in the conquest of the land of Palestine.

When we looked at Joshua we said that:

1. The people of the land were not fully faithful to God's promises.
2. The conquest of the land did not fully fulfil God's purposes.

In Hebrews 3 v 7 – 4 v 11, through an exposition of Psalm 95, the writer explores the significance of the land for Christian believers. He shows that the promise of rest still stands for these two reasons: because the people were not faithful and because the conquest under Joshua did not ultimately fulfil God's purposes.

1. The people of the land were not fully faithful to God's promises

The writer of Hebrews was writing to people who were tempted to turn back from Christ and return to Judaism. What Judaism offered was more tangible—the priesthood, the temple, the synagogue. In contrast, the unadorned gospel message of Christ, without signs and symbols, seemed insufficient with all its radical simplicity. And so the writer calls on his readers to consider the generation that failed to enter the land.

> **Hebrews 3 v 18 – 4 v 2**
>
> And to whom did God swear that they would never enter his rest if not to those who disobeyed? So we see that they were not able to enter, because of their unbelief.

Therefore, since the promise of entering his rest still stands, let us be careful that none of you be found to have fallen short of it. For we also have had the gospel preached to us, just as they did; but the message they heard was of no value to them, because those who heard did not combine it with faith.

They did not receive the rest of God because of their disobedience (3 v 18), and their disobedience lay in their failure to trust the word of God (3 v 19). They had the gospel preached to them but they did not combine it with faith (4 v 2).

Hebrews 4 v 6-11

It still remains that some will enter that rest, and those who formerly had the gospel preached to them did not go in, because of their disobedience. Therefore God again set a certain day, calling it Today, when a long time later he spoke through David, as was said before: "Today, if you hear his voice, do not harden your hearts." For if Joshua had given them rest, God would not have spoken later about another day. There remains, then, a Sabbath-rest for the people of God; for anyone who enters God's rest also rests from his own work, just as God did from his. Let us, therefore, make every effort to enter that rest, so that no-one will fall by following their example of disobedience.

The generation that rebelled in the desert did not enter God's rest. Because they turned from God, the promise was not fully fulfilled (4 v 6). Even Joshua could not give people the true rest (4 v 8) and so the promise of God's rest remains open (4 v 1). The invitation comes to us in the gospel (4 v 6). We who believe in Jesus can enter the rest of God (4 v 3) if we continue to hold on to Him (3 v 14).

2. The conquest of the land did not fully fulfil God's purposes

But it was not just the unfaithfulness of the people that meant the promise was not fully fulfilled under Joshua. The conquest of the land of Palestine—however complete—would not have fully fulfilled God's purposes. God's ultimate purpose is that we might share His eternal rest (Hebrews 4 v 4-5). God's purposes are not for a strip of land on the eastern shore of the Mediterranean, but for a whole new heaven and new earth. God's purpose is to mend the rend in the heavens and heal the earth. His plan is for the earth to enjoy liberation from its bondage and to enable it to fulfil His intentions in creation (Romans 8 v 19-21).

As the story of promise unfolds, the scope of the promise enlarges. Each partial fulfilment points beyond itself to God's ultimate purposes in Christ. In the Sermon on the Mount Jesus says: "Blessed are the meek, for they will inherit the earth" (Matthew 5 v 5). He is alluding to Psalm 37, which says: "The meek will inherit the land and enjoy great peace" (37 v 11). But notice that while in the psalm the meek inherit the *land,* Jesus now says that they inherit the *earth*. The promise of a land has expanded to become the promise of the earth.

Paul makes the same move in Romans 4. In emphasising that salvation is by faith he says: "It was not through law that Abraham and his offspring received the promise that he would be heir of the world, but through the righteousness that comes by faith" (Romans 4 v 13). But God's promise to Abraham was: "To your offspring I will give this land" (Genesis 12 v 7). Just as Abraham's offspring are not his genetic descendants, but those from all nations who share his faith, so the promise of a land finds its ultimate fulfilment in a world made new for God's new humanity.

The church: in Christ

What happens to the theme of the land in the New Testament? The place where blessing is found is "in Christ". "In Christ" is a characteristic phrase of Paul, although other New Testament writers also use it. Sometimes Paul appears to use it simply as a synonym for "Christian" (a term he does not use). But often it has a clear sense of a location or sphere, which, through faith, believers have entered. "In Christ" is the location in which the promised blessing and rest can be found. But it is more than a location, since it transcends geography. It refers to what Christ has done on our behalf. Although the New Testament also uses the phrase "in the LORD", the predominant phrase is "in Christ" or "in Christ Jesus". This suggests that it should be seen in messianic terms ("Christ" is the Greek term for the Hebrew word "Messiah"). To be "in Christ" is to be part of the messianic realm Christ has inaugurated.

A salvation reality

"In Christ" refers to a salvation reality (2 Timothy 2 v 10). Through our union with Christ, His death and resurrection become our death to sin and our life to God; they become our redemption and justification. In Adam humanity was expelled from Eden because of his disobedience. Now the new humanity in Christ find salvation through His righteousness (2 Corinthians 15 v 21-22). "In Christ" we are sanctified (1 Corinthians 1 v 2). Christ becomes our righteousness, holiness and wisdom (1 Corinthians 1 v 30). In Christ there is a new creation in which God has reconciled the world to Himself (2 Corinthians 5 v 17-19).

To be "in Christ" is to be in a place or sphere of freedom (Galatians 2 v 4), blessing (Ephesians 1 v 3), peace (Philippians 4 v 7) and provision (Philippians 4 v 19; Philemon 6). It is a location near to God for both Jew and Gentile (Ephesians 2 v 13). So to be in Christ is to be in a place of blessing, peace and provision in which God is near—this is the fulfilment of the land of promise.

A communal reality

"In Christ" is also a communal reality (Romans 12 v 4-5; Galatians 3 v 26-29). The salvation we have in Christ is corporate. Paul speaks of those who are in Christ as a synonym for churches. The theme of the land is expressed in the community of the church. The land was a place of provision and this provision extended to all as the people lived according to God's law—a way of life that matched their experience of redemption and as recipients of the land as a gift from God. The church also practised generosity and sharing in a way that reflected their status as redeemed people and inheritors of a new creation. In this way the early church was able to provide for all in need (Acts 2 v 44-45; 4 v 32-35). When Luke says of the early church that "there were no needy persons among them" (Acts 4 v 34), he is echoing Deuteronomy 15:

> **Deuteronomy 15 v 4-5**
> However, there should be no poor among you, for in the land the LORD your God is giving you to possess as your inheritance, he will richly bless you, if only you fully obey the LORD your God and are careful to follow all these commands I am giving you today.

There are no needy people in the place of God's blessing—whether the land or those in Christ—when God's people live in joyful obedience to Him.

A future reality

Finally, "in Christ" refers also to a future reality (Philippians 3 v 14; 1 Peter 5:10). Peter speaks of an inheritance which is kept in heaven for us and for which we are kept by God's power (1 Peter 1 v 3-5). It is the idea of an inheritance in the land. But our inheritance is not in the land of Palestine, but in the new creation.

> **Ephesians 1 v 13-14**
> And you also were included in Christ when you heard the word of truth, the gospel of your salvation. Having believed, you were marked in him with a seal, the promised Holy Spirit, who is a deposit guaranteeing our inheritance until the redemption of those who are God's possession—to the praise of his glory.

The Israelites listened to the accounts of the allocation of the land with interest because they were waiting for confirmation of their entitlement to their inheritance in the land of blessing. In the same way we have received the title deeds of our glorious inheritance in the form of the Holy Spirit. The Spirit is the guarantee of our coming inheritance. Indeed, through the Spirit we experience together something of that future reality already in history. The church is the community of the Holy Spirit (2 Corinthians 13 v 14)—the community of the coming age.

New Creation: the promised New Creation

In Revelation 21 – 22 John describes the ultimate fulfilment of the promise to Abraham of a land—the promise that was realised through the death and resurrection of Jesus Christ. He sees a new heaven and a new earth. The fulfilment of the promise of a land is ultimately cosmic in scope. God is going to restore the entire creation. It is a place without threat, which in John's imagery is symbolised by the absence of any sea (21 v 1). It is a place where God meets with His people (21 v 3). And it is a place of blessing without death, mourning, crying or pain (21 v 4).

But John also picks up the imagery of a new Jerusalem (21 v 2). Like Ezekiel before him, John is shown a wonderful new city (21 v 10-21).

Revelation 22 v 1-3

Then the angel showed me the river of the water of life, as clear as crystal, flowing from the throne of God and of the Lamb down the middle of the great street of the city. On each side of the river stood the tree of life, bearing twelve crops of fruit, yielding its fruit every month. And the leaves of the tree are for the healing of the nations. No longer will there be any curse. The throne of God and of the Lamb will be in the city, and his servants will serve him.

We have seen this imagery already. It is the language of Ezekiel 47 and, beyond Ezekiel, it is the language of Eden restored. Like Ezekiel, John sees a river of water, on each side of which is "the tree of life", bearing fruit each month and bearing leaves for the healing of the nations (22 v 1-2). Once again we have access to the tree of life. The river flows from the throne of the Lamb, for it is the reign of the crucified one that brings life to the land (22 v 1). At the very end of the story we discover that Jesus Christ is the tree of life. It is Christ who gives us life. He has removed the curse of the fall by His death on our behalf (22 v 3). God's ultimate purpose is a new humanity with God in a new creation.

Conclusion

What does the promise of a land mean for us? It means what it meant to Abraham. The promise to Abraham was the gospel announced in advance (Galatians 3 v 8). God promised Abraham a land of blessing and that promise became central in determining Abraham's life. In the gospel God promises us not just a land, but a new creation, and that promise should be central in determining our lives.

Hebrews 11 v 8-10, 13-16

By faith Abraham, when called to go to a place he would later receive as his inheritance, obeyed and went, even though he did not know where he was going. By faith he made his home in the promised land like a stranger in a foreign country; he lived in tents, as did Isaac and Jacob, who were heirs with him of the same promise. For he was looking forward to the city with foundations, whose architect and builder is God...

All these people were still living by faith when they died. They did not receive the things promised; they only saw them and welcomed them from a distance. And they admitted that they were aliens and strangers on earth. People who say such things show that they are looking for a country of their own. If they had been thinking of the country they had left, they would have had opportunity to return. Instead, they were longing for a better country—a heavenly one. Therefore God is not ashamed to be called their God, for he has prepared a city for them.

The writer of Hebrews emphasises that Abraham and his descendants did not receive what was promised. They died still waiting for it. They welcomed it only from a distance.

They longed for something better. They were aliens and strangers. Abraham was living by the promise of God. The solid thing in his life—the thing that he had received—was the promise of God. And that promise pointed him to a city with foundations whose architect and builder is God; a heavenly city prepared by God (see John 14 v 2).

And this, says the writer of Hebrews, is what faith is. Faith is looking forward to something better. This is not simply wishful thinking, for we have received the promise of God. Faith is living by the promise of God. God has promised us a better place and so we think of ourselves as foreigners and strangers. "Our citizenship is in heaven" (Philippians 3 v 20). We do not belong in this world. Our hearts are set on a heavenly city, prepared for us by God (1 Peter 1 v 1, 3-5; 2 v 11).

***

Case Study: the promise of a land and the book of Nehemiah

How does the theme of God's promise of a place of blessing help us understand the message of Nehemiah for Christians today?

Under the leadership of Nehemiah the people are able to rebuild the walls of Jerusalem. But Nehemiah cannot give them rest from their enemies. The book is in two halves: the first is about the rebuilding of the temple and the second is about the reform of the people. Nehemiah 6 v 15-16 feels as if it ought be the climax of the first half.

Nehemiah 6 v 15-16
So the wall was completed on the twenty-fifth of Elul, in fifty-two days. When all our enemies heard about this, all

the surrounding nations were afraid and lost their self-confidence, because they realised that this work had been done with the help of our God.

The wall has been rebuilt, despite opposition, in just fifty-two days. But the first half of the book actually ends with 6 v 17 – 7 v 3.

Nehemiah 6 v 17 – 7 v 3
Also, in those days the nobles of Judah were sending many letters to Tobiah, and replies from Tobiah kept coming to them. For many in Judah were under oath to him, since he was son-in-law to Shecaniah son of Arah, and his son Jehohanan had married the daughter of Meshullam son of Berekiah. Moreover, they kept reporting to me his good deeds and then telling him what I said. And Tobiah sent letters to intimidate me.

After the wall had been rebuilt and I had set the doors in place, the gatekeepers and the singers and the Levites were appointed. I put in charge of Jerusalem my brother Hanani, along with Hananiah the commander of the citadel, because he was a man of integrity and feared God more than most men do. I said to them, "The gates of Jerusalem are not to be opened until the sun is hot. While the gatekeepers are still on duty, make them shut the doors and bar them. Also appoint residents of Jerusalem as guards, some at their posts and some near their own houses."

These verses form a kind of anticlimax to the rebuilding of Jerusalem. Nehemiah has not brought rest in the promised land. The land is still a place of threat and struggle.

We are left waiting for One who will say: "Come to me ...

and I will give you rest" (Matthew 11 v 28). It is in Christ that we find the hope of security, liberation, provision and blessing. The writer of Hebrews calls on us to "make every effort to enter that rest" through faith in the gospel (Hebrews 4 v 11). And in the church we anticipate the inheritance that is ours in Christ as we provide a place of security and blessing for one another.

Chapter 4

The promise of a King and a kingdom

Figure 24: The promise of a King and a kingdom: Outline

Creation	God rules through His word
Fall	God's rule rejected
Abraham	God rules through a promise *God's law given to the redeemed, not to redeem* *God's law given to bless, not to restrict*
Israel	God rules through His king
Into exile	God rules through the prophetic word
Prophecy	God will rule through the coming King
Jesus	The promised Saviour King: *The kingdom comes now in hidden, gracious* *way through God's word* *The kingdom will come in glory and triumph*
The church	King Jesus rules through the gospel
New creation	An everlasting rule of freedom

What do you think of when you hear the words "rule" and "government"? Along with any positive associations we may have, when we think of "rule" we commonly think of tyranny, oppression, pride, corruption, pomp and self-aggrandisement. We live in an age that is suspicious of authority. For us, rule and freedom are opposites. We might recognise the need to give up some freedom for the sake of others or for our security—rule may bring benefits. But any benefits come at the price of freedom. Yet this is how Mark says that Jesus began His ministry:

Mark 1 v 14-15
After John was put in prison, Jesus went into Galilee, proclaiming the good news of God. "The time has come," he said. "The kingdom of God is near. Repent and believe the good news!"

Jesus proclaimed good news and the good news was that the kingdom of God was near. The word "kingdom" means "rule", "reign", "government" or "sovereignty". God's reign was near and Jesus assumed this was good news.

Creation: God rules through his word

Who is in charge of the world?

Genesis 1 v 1-3
In the beginning God created the heavens and the earth. Now the earth was formless and empty, darkness was over the surface of the deep, and the Spirit of God was hovering over the waters.

And God said, "Let there be light," and there was light.

God is in charge. This is not such an obvious statement as it first seems. The account of Genesis was written in a context of polytheism. There were many gods on offer. Each nation had its own deity; most had several. It is not so very different today with our religious pluralism and competing ideologies. Israel was just one nation among many with one God among many. Yet in the opening chapter of the Bible a staggering claim is made. The book of Genesis claims that Israel's God, Yahweh, the God of Abraham, Isaac and Jacob, is the one Creator God. He is the absolute sovereign of the universe. What is being asserted in these verses is the reign of God. "The earth is the LORD's, and everything in it, the world, and all who live in it" (Psalm 24 v 1). Who reigns? God reigns.

How does God reign? How does God create this world? "And God said, 'Let there be light,' and there was light" (Genesis 1 v 3). He simply speaks and the universe comes into being. He rules through His word (see John 1 v 1-3).

What is humanity's role?

Genesis 1 v 27-28
So God created man in his own image, in the image of God he created him; male and female he created them. God blessed them and said to them, "Be fruitful and increase in number; fill the earth and subdue it. Rule over the fish of the sea and the birds of the air and over every living creature that moves on the ground."

God places Adam and Eve in the garden. They are to live under God's rule. And they are to rule with God over creation: "Rule over the fish of the sea and the birds of the air and over every living creature that moves on the ground" (Genesis 1 v 28). Humanity was to rule God's world under God's authority.

What is God's rule like?
Genesis 2 v 8-9, 15-17
Now the LORD God had planted a garden in the east, in Eden; and there he put the man he had formed. And the LORD God made all kinds of trees grow out of the ground—trees that were pleasing to the eye and good for food. In the middle of the garden were the tree of life and the tree of the knowledge of good and evil.

The LORD God took the man and put him in the Garden of Eden to work it and take care of it. And the LORD God commanded the man, "You are free to eat from any tree in the garden; but you must not eat from the tree of the knowledge of good and evil, for when you eat of it you will surely die."

God's rule is a rule of blessing and prosperity, peace and freedom. Adam and Eve are to express their commitment to God's rule through trust in His word. Again we see that God rules through this word.

Fall: God's rule is rejected
Genesis 3 v 1-6
Now the serpent was more crafty than any of the wild animals the LORD God had made. He said to the woman, "Did God really say, 'You must not eat from any tree in the garden'?"

The woman said to the serpent, "We may eat fruit from the trees in the garden, but God did say, 'You must not eat fruit from the tree that is in the middle of the garden, and you must not touch it, or you will die.'"

"You will not surely die," the serpent said to the woman. "For God knows that when you eat of it your eyes will be opened, and you will be like God, knowing good and evil."

When the woman saw that the fruit of the tree was good for food and pleasing to the eye, and also desirable for gaining wisdom, she took some and ate it. She also gave some to her husband, who was with her, and he ate it.

Humanity rejects God's rule. But notice how this is done. The serpent encourages the woman to doubt God's word (3 v 1) and then deny God's word (3 v 4). The achievement of the serpent—if "achievement" is the right word—is to stop the woman trusting God's word and obeying God's word. Instead of trusting the word of God, the woman is governed by what seems "pleasing to the eye" (3 v 6). God rules as His word is trusted and obeyed. But now His word is not trusted and not obeyed. Humanity has rejected God's rule.

But not only has the serpent got humanity to reject God's rule, he has redefined the whole notion of rule. The rule of God was a rule of love, peace, freedom, blessing and life. The serpent portrays it as oppressive and tyrannical. And we have modelled human rule in the image of the serpent's lie. We think of rule as oppressive because human rule *is* so often oppressive. Revolutions start out with good intentions, but time and again they become as tyrannical as the regimes that they replaced. Our ideas of what it means to rule or to be ruled are not shaped by God's good rule, but by the lie of Satan.

This is important. The Bible is the story of God re-establishing His rule—His rule that brings life, salvation, peace and justice. But all the time we are hostile to God's rule because we think it will tyrannise us. We reject God's rule because we will not trust His word. God has to redefine what rule is (see Mark 10 v 40-45).

Human rule becomes oppressive

Humanity's rule becomes oppressive. We rule over creation not as God rules—in a way that brings blessing, freedom and life. We rule in the image of Satan's lie. We tyrannise the earth, we pollute and destroy. Our generation is reaping the seeds of humanity's destructive rule over the earth.

Human rule becomes subverted

At the same time as we are exploiting creation, we are being ruled by creation. The order of creation is reversed. Humanity was to rule over the animals, but in Genesis 3 the serpent rules over humanity. Think about drug misuse: instead of ruling over the plants, we are ruled by the hop or the poppy.

Human rule becomes conflict ridden

If I claim to be the ruler of my life, what happens when I come into contact with you? Who will be ruler? The result is conflict and envy. We see it right away in Genesis 4 when Cain's jealousy and hatred leads to his murder of Abel.

Abraham: God rules through a promise

In Genesis 12 God promises Abraham a "nation"—the word suggests a political entity ruled over by a king. God says to Abraham: "I will make nations of you, and kings will come from you" (Genesis 17 v 6). This promise of kings anticipates the promise to David. But before David there are only hints at the central role of God's King.

Think instead about what a promise is. A promise is a word and it is a word about the future. It is this future orientation that gives the promise of God its redemptive character. It is not a statement of what is, but a statement of what will be. When God makes His promise to Abraham, Abraham acts in accordance with that promise. The promise governs his action. He sets out from Ur and spends his life in tents. The word of God rules his life. God is beginning to re-establish His rule through His word. This promise shapes the story of the whole Bible and drives the story forward. Events happen in accordance with the promise. When God liberates His people from Egypt, He does so because of His promise to Abraham (Exodus 2 v 23-25; 3 v 15; 6 v 8).

When God liberates Israel from Egypt, He gives a word in the form of a law. The promise to Abraham is re-stated in the covenant made through Moses. This law is to govern—notice the language of rule—the life of God's redeemed people.

1. God's law is given to redeemed people, not to redeem
"And God spoke all these words: 'I am the LORD your God, who brought you out of Egypt, out of the land of slavery'" (Exodus 20 v 1-2). The people would not be saved by obeying God's law. The law of Sinai was not given as a means of salvation. It was given to people who had already been redeemed in the exodus.

Law and gospel were not intended to be opposites. The law of Moses points forward to the gospel of Jesus Christ. The law of Moses was the word by which God ruled His people as they waited for the coming Saviour. The law of Moses was not Plan A that went wrong, forcing God to come up with Plan B in Jesus. The law finds its fulfilment in the gospel. Law and gospel only become opposites when people see the law as the means of salvation. It is salvation by works and salvation by faith that are opposites. The saints of the Old Testament had faith in that to which the law pointed—the promised Saviour—and that was saving faith. Trusting the law and living accordingly brought salvation, just as trusting the gospel does. And that is very different from thinking that you could be right with God by obeying the law. The problem came when people saw the law of Moses as a means of salvation instead of as a pointer to a greater exodus.

2. God's law is given to bless, not to restrict

Sometimes we think God's law is there to stop us having a good time. But the psalmist had a very different perspective: "Your law is my delight ... Oh, how I love your law!" (Psalm 119 v 77, 97). God's rule brings life, blessing, peace and justice. God rules through His word. The law of Moses was the word by which He would rule Israel. Hence the psalmist's delight in God's law. God's law is God's word, which is God's rule. It is a word of liberation and a word of blessing.

Obedience to God's word does not bring loss, but liberation. It is not that we must put up with the restrictions of God's law until the day of liberation. It is not that the benefits of following God outweigh the pleasures we miss out on. The rule of God *is* the blessing. This is where freedom and blessing are found—under the rule of God expressed in His law. We see this time and again in the law itself. The Israelites had been liberated from the oppressive rule of Pharaoh. Now they were to live a way of complete contrast—a way of liberation.

When the nations saw Israel living according to God's law, they would not say: "Look at those killjoys, oppressed by the moral code of their god."

Figure 25: Pharaoh's rule and God's rule

Pharaoh's rule	God's exodus rule
The powerful have complete power over others	God's authority prevents people claiming complete power (Deut. 5 v 7)
The gods are used to support the powerful	An imageless God cannot be co-opted and the divine name cannot be used for gain (Deut. 5 v 8-11)
Production and consumption is unrestrained	The Sabbath sets limits to production and consumption (Deut. 5 v 12-15)
Vulnerable workers are exploited and overworked	Rest for all with protection for vulnerable workers (Deut. 5 v 12-15)
Family life is subject to destructive interference	Respect for paternal authority and marital integrity (Deut. 5 v 16,18)
The weak are vulnerable to violence with state-organised genocide	Respect for human life (Deut. 5 v 17)
The weak are vulnerable to economic exploitation	The weak are protected from the greed of the powerful (Deut. 5 v 19, 21)
The weak have no effective legal protection	Integrity and impartiality of judicial system (Deut. 5 v 20)

Deuteronomy 4 v 6-8

Observe [these decrees and laws] carefully, for this will show your wisdom and understanding to the nations, who will hear about all these decrees and say, "Surely this great nation is a wise and understanding people." What other nation is so great as to have their gods near them the way the LORD our God is near us whenever we pray to him? And what other nation is so great as to have such righteous decrees and laws as this body of laws I am setting before you today?

We are given a lovely example of God's liberating law in action in the book of Ruth. The story of Ruth gives a snapshot of life under the rule of God. We see a vulnerable, immigrant widow finding blessing, peace and hope among the community of God's people as they live in accordance with His law. This is life under God's rule as God intended it to be.

Psalm 1 beautifully captures the sense that the word of God brings blessing and prosperity:

Psalm 1 v 1-3
Blessed is the man who does not walk in the counsel of the wicked or stand in the way of sinners or sit in the seat of mockers. But his delight is in the law of the LORD, and on his law he meditates day and night. He is like a tree planted by streams of water, which yields its fruit in season and whose leaf does not wither. Whatever he does prospers.

Israel: God rules through His King

When Israel began life in the promised land, it was ruled by God through His word. But time and again the people did not walk in the way of obedience to the LORD's commands. They would not accept the rule of God's word and so God judged them by handing them over to the surrounding nations. When Israel cried out in repentance, He sent leaders, called judges, to rescue them.

Judges 2 v 16-18

Then the LORD raised up judges, who saved them out of the hands of these raiders. Yet they would not listen to their judges but prostituted themselves to other gods and worshipped them. Unlike their fathers, they quickly turned from the way in which their fathers had walked, the way of obedience to the LORD's commands. Whenever the LORD raised up a judge for them, he was with the judge and saved them out of the hands of their enemies as long as the judge lived; for the LORD had compassion on them as they groaned under those who oppressed and afflicted them.

The key point is that the LORD was with the judges and the LORD saves Israel: "Whenever the LORD raised up a judge for them, he was with the judge and saved them out of the hands of their enemies" (Judges 2 v 18). The judges themselves were a motley crew: Ehud was left-handed and Deborah was a woman, which might have disqualified them from leadership in the culture of their day (Judges 3 – 5). Gideon was a coward (Judges 6 – 7) and Jephthah made a rash vow (Judges 10 – 11). Then there was Samson, whose every act of deliverance was initiated by his lust (Judges 13 – 16). None is a conventional hero, demonstrating that behind them was God. He is the true Judge, the true King and the true hero of the story. In Judges 11 v 27 Jephthah speaks of "the LORD, the Judge".

The closing line of the book of the Judges is: "In those days Israel had no king; everyone did as he saw fit" (Judges 21 v 25). This statement is to be read at different levels—it is both true and false:

It is true: Israel has no king

Gideon is offered the throne, but refuses it (Judges 8 v 22 –

23). And yet he names his son "Abimelech", which means "the king is my father" (Judges 8 v 31). Gideon himself acts like a greedy king, leading the people astray (Judges 8 v 24-27), while Abimelech's claim to be king leads to civil war and his own destruction (Judges 9).

It is false: Israel has a King

Israel has no human king because Israel has a divine King. God is the King of Israel. God rules His people.

It is true: Israel has no king

The problem is that Israel does not acknowledge her King: "everyone did as he saw fit" (Judges 21 v 25). The final chapters of the book of Judges portray life in a world of moral relativity—a very contemporary situation—and it is not pleasant. Life outside the rule of God is not a life of freedom and blessing. The contrast with the book of Ruth—written during the time of the judges—is striking.

It is perhaps no surprise, then, when the people come to Samuel, the last of the judges, and ask for a king.

> **1 Samuel 8 v 4-5**
> So all the elders of Israel gathered together and came to Samuel at Ramah. They said to him, "You are old, and your sons do not walk in your ways; now appoint a king to lead us, such as all the other nations have."

One problem with this request is immediately apparent: the people want a king "such as all the other nations have". They were called by God to be a light to the nations, but instead they want to be "like the nations". But the problem is deeper than that, for the people already have a King—God Himself. What they are saying is that they want a king *instead* of God.

God says to Samuel: "It is not you they have rejected, but they have rejected me as their king" (1 Samuel 8 v 7).

Samuel warns the people what sort of a king they will get. He will take their sons to serve in his army. He will take their daughters to serve in his court. He will take their wealth for his own needs. But the people want their king (1 Samuel 8 v 10-20). When Samuel gives his farewell address to the people, he reminds them that he has not exploited or extorted anything from them. The implication is clear: the king you have asked for will do so. He reminds them of all God has done for them. Again the implication is clear: God's rule has been good, but now they have chosen another king. God sends a terrible thunderstorm that destroys the wheat harvest to show "what an evil thing you did in the eyes of the LORD when you asked for a king" (1 Samuel 12 v 17).

Samuel is the last judge and the first member of the prophetic order. There had been prophets before—Moses and Deborah are described as such. But the prophet as an institution arises with the monarchy. The king is to rule under God's rule, expressed through His word. That is what God said in Deuteronomy 17 when He anticipated the people's request for a king. The prophets proclaim this word. The prophet guides the king so that the king rules under God's authority. That is the ideal. More often, however, the prophet keeps the king in check, calling him back to God's word. Often the word of the prophet and the rule of the king are in conflict.

We see this conflict in the reign of the first king, Saul. Saul gets off to a good start, but soon it all unravels. Saul is told to destroy the Amalekites and all their possessions, but he saves the best of the sheep and oxen for sacrifice. Samuel says that God has rejected Saul as king because what counts is not sacrifice, but obedience to God's word.

1 Samuel 15 v 22-23

Samuel replied: "Does the LORD delight in burnt offerings and sacrifices as much as in obeying the voice of the LORD? To obey is better than sacrifice, and to heed is better than the fat of rams. For rebellion is like the sin of divination, and arrogance like the evil of idolatry. Because you have rejected the word of the LORD, he has rejected you as king."

God rejects Saul because Saul rejects God's word. So in 1 Samuel 16 another king is chosen—David. David is anointed as the next king. The word "Christ" in Greek or "Messiah" in Hebrew means "anointed one". Israelite kings were not crowned, but anointed with oil. So "the Christ" is God's anointed King. David is, in a very real sense, the christ. He is God's anointed king at that time.

But for years David must live at the margins, a fugitive on the run from Saul. He does not seize the kingdom by force—even when he has the opportunity to kill Saul—but was given it by God (1 Samuel 24; 26). Even when he becomes king he suffers from the rebellion of other nations and the rebellion of his own family. He expresses that suffering in laments in the book of Psalms. David is the christ who suffers.

When David comes to the throne, the story takes a surprising turn. It does not appear surprising to us because we have grown used to Christmas readings about Jesus being descended from David. But remember that the request for a king was "an evil thing" (1 Samuel 12 v 17).

2 Samuel 7 v 1-17

After the king was settled in his palace and the LORD had given him rest from all his enemies around him, he said to

Nathan the prophet, "Here I am, living in a palace of cedar, while the ark of God remains in a tent."

Nathan replied to the king, "Whatever you have in mind, go ahead and do it, for the LORD is with you." That night the word of the LORD came to Nathan, saying: "Go and tell my servant David, 'This is what the LORD says:

'Are you the one to build me a house to dwell in? I have not dwelt in a house from the day I brought the Israelites up out of Egypt to this day. I have been moving from place to place with a tent as my dwelling. Wherever I have moved with all the Israelites, did I ever say to any of their rulers whom I commanded to shepherd my people Israel, "Why have you not built me a house of cedar?"'

"Now then, tell my servant David, 'This is what the LORD Almighty says: I took you from the pasture and from following the flock to be ruler over my people Israel. I have been with you wherever you have gone, and I have cut off all your enemies from before you. Now I will make your name great, like the names of the greatest men of the earth. And I will provide a place for my people Israel and will plant them so that they can have a home of their own and no longer be disturbed. Wicked people shall not oppress them any more, as they did at the beginning and have done ever since the time I appointed leaders over my people Israel. I will also give you rest from all your enemies.

"'The LORD declares to you that the LORD himself will establish a house for you: When your days are over and you rest with your fathers, I will raise up your offspring to succeed you, who will come from your own body, and I will establish his kingdom. He is the one who will build a house for my Name, and I will establish the throne of his kingdom for ever. I will be his father, and he shall be my son. When he does wrong, I will punish him with the rod of men, with floggings inflicted by men. But my love will never be taken away from him, as I took it away from Saul, whom I removed from before you. Your house and your kingdom shall endure for ever before me; your throne shall be established for ever.'"

Nathan reported to David all the words of this entire revelation.

David wants to build a temple for God. God's ark is in a tent while David now has a palace of cedar. It is a good instinct and the prophet Nathan commends the proposal. But God has another plan. For one thing God does not need a house to live in. Indeed, the God on the move (2 Samuel 7 v 6) will not "rest" in a temple until He has given His people "rest" from their enemies (2 Samuel 7 v 11). Furthermore, what can David do for God? David was a peasant shepherd until God made him king.

David wanted to build a house (temple) for God. Instead God is going to build a house (dynasty) for David—one that will last forever. David's house may go astray, but God will never remove His love from it. When the people asked for a king, it was an evil request because they rejected God as their king. But now that evil act is woven into the plan of salvation. God will rule through His anointed King.

After David has committed adultery with Bathsheba and had her husband killed, Nathan the prophet exposes him and says: "Out of your own household I am going to bring calamity upon you" (2 Samuel 12 v 11). Here is the word "house" again. David wanted to a build a "house" (temple) for God. Instead God will give David an everlasting "house" (dynasty). But now there will be conflict in David's "house" (family). His son Amnon rapes his half-sister, Tamar. Tamar's brother, Absalom, murders Amnon. Absalom later rebels against David, but is killed. All the time we are asking: Which son will inherit the promise? Who will be the son of David on the throne of David?

Eventually Solomon succeeds and Israel reaches its height. We see God's king ruling in God's way and it is glorious. But Solomon turns from God and we see the signs of decay. In Deuteronomy 17 v 14-17 Moses says that the king should not:

- acquire great numbers of horses
- return to Egypt to get them
- marry many wives
- accumulate large quantities of gold

In 1 Kings 10 v 14 – 11 v 3 we see Solomon breaking each of these commands.

Solomon is succeeded by Rehoboam. Rehoboam follows the advice of young hotheads and oppresses the people. Jeroboam leads a rebellion and the kingdom divides into two. The ten northern tribes break off and become known as Israel. The Davidic line continues to rule over the two southern tribes of Judah and Benjamin, usually known as simply as Judah.

In the northern kingdom we get a succession of bloody coups (1 Kings 15 – 16). Whole families are slaughtered so that no dynasty is established. The dynasties of the northern kingdom come to nothing. Ultimately, the kingdom itself comes to nothing. It is defeated by the Assyrians, exiled and extinguished from history.

In the southern kingdom the dynasty of David continues.

1 Kings 15 v 1-4
In the eighteenth year of the reign of Jeroboam son of Nebat,
Abijah became king of Judah, and he reigned in Jerusalem
for three years. His mother's name was Maacah daughter of
Abishalom.

He committed all the sins his father had done before him;
his heart was not fully devoted to the LORD his God, as the
heart of David his forefather had been. Nevertheless, for
David's sake the LORD his God gave him a lamp in Jerusalem
by raising up a son to succeed him and by making Jerusalem
strong.

David's line continues—despite its sin—because of God's
promise to David. It is only the power of God's word that
preserves David's line and its movement towards fulfilment
in Jesus Christ. God's plan of salvation is now tied to the
family of David.

Decline into exile: God rules through the prophetic word

In the Hebrew canon the history books of the Old Testament
(Joshua to 2 Kings) are called the Former Prophets. The main
force in these books is not the kings or the international
powers, but the word of the Lord that comes by the mouth
of His prophets. To understand the story you must listen to
Samuel, Nathan, Elijah and so on. The central theme of 1
and 2 Kings is the sovereignty and certainty of God's word.
When the word of God comes into conflict with the king, it
is God's word that reigns.

1 Kings 13 v 1-6

By the word of the LORD a man of God came from Judah to Bethel, as Jeroboam was standing by the altar to make an offering. He cried out against the altar by the word of the LORD: "O altar, altar! This is what the LORD says: 'A son named Josiah will be born to the house of David. On you he will sacrifice the priests of the high places who now make offerings here, and human bones will be burned on you.'" That same day the man of God gave a sign: "This is the sign the LORD has declared: The altar will be split apart and the ashes on it will be poured out."

When King Jeroboam heard what the man of God cried out against the altar at Bethel, he stretched out his hand from the altar and said, "Seize him!" But the hand he stretched out towards the man shrivelled up, so that he could not pull it back. Also, the altar was split apart and its ashes poured out according to the sign given by the man of God by the word of the LORD.

Then the king said to the man of God, "Intercede with the LORD your God and pray for me that my hand may be restored." So the man of God interceded with the LORD, and the king's hand was restored and became as it was before.

This is part of a section that begins "By the word of the LORD" and ends "the word of the LORD … will certainly come true" (1 Kings 13 v 32). An un-named man of God comes to Jeroboam to predict the downfall of the golden calves Jeroboam has erected. Jeroboam tries to stop the prophet, as if by doing so he could stop God's word operating. He pits his authority against the authority of God's word. He tries to turn back God's word, like King Canute trying to turn back the tide. It cannot be done and his outstretched hand shrivels up. God does His work through His word. God's word drives the story. It determines events. It not only informs, warns and predicts—it actually causes things to happen.

1 Kings 13 v 7-32

The king said to the man of God, "Come home with me and have something to eat, and I will give you a gift."

But the man of God answered the king, "Even if you were to give me half your possessions, I would not go with you, nor would I eat bread or drink water here. For I was commanded by the word of the LORD: "You must not eat bread or drink water or return by the way you came.'" So he took another road and did not return by the way he had come to Bethel.

Now there was a certain old prophet living in Bethel, whose sons came and told him all that the man of God had done there that day. They also told their father what he had said to the king. Their father asked them, "Which way did he go?" And his sons showed him which road the man of God from Judah had taken. So he said to his sons, "Saddle the donkey for me." And when they had saddled the donkey for him, he mounted it and rode after the man of God. He found him sitting under an oak tree and asked, 'Are you the man of God who came from Judah?'"

"I am," he replied. So the prophet said to him, "Come home with me and eat."

The man of God said, "I cannot turn back and go with you, nor can I eat bread or drink water with you in this place. I have been told by the word of the LORD: 'You must not eat bread or drink water there or return by the way you came.'"

The old prophet answered, "I too am a prophet, as you are. And an angel said to me by the word of the LORD: 'Bring him back with you to your house so that he may eat bread and drink water.'" (But he was lying to him.) So the man of God returned with him and ate and drank in his house.

While they were sitting at the table, the word of the LORD came to the old prophet who had brought him back. He cried out to the man of God who had come from Judah, "This is what the LORD says: 'You have defied the word of the LORD and have not kept the command the LORD your God gave you. You came back and ate bread and drank water in the place where he told you not to eat or drink. Therefore your body will not be buried in the tomb of your fathers.'"

When the man of God had finished eating and drinking, the prophet who had brought him back saddled his donkey for him. As he went on his way, a lion met him on the road and killed him, and his body was thrown down on the road, with both the donkey and the lion standing beside it. Some people who passed by saw the body thrown down there, with the lion standing beside the body, and they went and reported it in the city where the old prophet lived.

When the prophet who had brought him back from his journey heard of it, he said, "It is the man of God who defied the word of the LORD. The LORD has given him over to the lion, which has mauled him and killed him, as the word of the LORD had warned him."

The prophet said to his sons, "Saddle the donkey for me," and they did so. Then he went out and found the body thrown down on the road, with the donkey and the lion standing beside it. The lion had neither eaten the body nor mauled the donkey. So the prophet picked up the body of the man of God, laid it on the donkey, and brought it back to his own city to mourn for him and bury him. Then he laid the body in his own tomb, and they mourned over him and said, "Oh, my brother!"

After burying him, he said to his sons, "When I die, bury me in the grave where the man of God is buried; lay my bones beside his bones. For the message he declared by the word of the LORD against the altar in Bethel and against all the shrines on the high places in the towns of Samaria will certainly come true."

It is not clear why the man of God from Judah is not to eat or drink on his return journey. Still less are we told why the prophet of Bethel decides to trick the man from Judah into eating with him. What is clear is that the prophet tragically becomes an illustration of his own message. God's word is certain. Even though the man of God from Judah cannot be held culpable, because he was tricked, he still dies in fulfilment of God's word (1 Kings 13 v 26). How much more certain is God's word of judgment against Jeroboam (1 Kings 13 v 32).

This pattern of conflict between the king and the prophet is repeated throughout the stories of Israel's kings, with the word of God proving to be sovereign.

2 Kings 1 v 1-8
After Ahab's death, Moab rebelled against Israel. Now

Ahaziah had fallen through the lattice of his upper room in Samaria and injured himself. So he sent messengers, saying to them, "Go and consult Baal-zebub, the god of Ekron, to see if I will recover from this injury."

But the angel of the LORD said to Elijah the Tishbite, "Go up and meet the messengers of the king of Samaria and ask them, 'Is it because there is no God in Israel that you are going off to consult Baal-zebub, the god of Ekron?' Therefore this is what the LORD says: 'You will not leave the bed you are lying on. You will certainly die!'" So Elijah went.

When the messengers returned to the king, he asked them, "Why have you come back?"

"A man came to meet us," they replied. "And he said to us, 'Go back to the king who sent you and tell him, "This is what the LORD says: Is it because there is no God in Israel that you are sending men to consult Baal-zebub, the god of Ekron? Therefore you will not leave the bed you are lying on. You will certainly die!"'"

The king asked them, "What kind of man was it who came to meet you and told you this?" They replied, "He was a man with a garment of hair and with a leather belt round his waist." The king said, "That was Elijah the Tishbite."

Ahaziah seems to think that he will get a better word from Baal than from God. He is probably right. He has "provoked the LORD" by his worship of Baal (1 Kings 22 v 53). Ahaziah seems to think he can avoid God's word if he avoids God's prophet.

2 Kings 1 v 9-17

Then he sent to Elijah a captain with his company of fifty men. The captain went up to Elijah, who was sitting on the top of a hill, and said to him, "Man of God, the king says, 'Come down!'"

Elijah answered the captain, "If I am a man of God, may fire come down from heaven and consume you and your fifty men!" Then the fire fell from heaven and consumed the captain and his men.

At this the king sent to Elijah another captain with his fifty men. The captain said to him, "Man of God, this is what the king says, 'Come down at once!'"

"If I am a man of God," Elijah replied, "may fire come down from heaven and consume you and your fifty men!" Then the fire of God fell from heaven and consumed him and his fifty men.

So the king sent a third captain with his fifty men. This third captain went up and fell on his knees before Elijah. "Man of God," he begged, "please have respect for my life and the lives of these fifty men, your servants! See, fire has fallen from heaven and consumed the first two captains and all their men. But now have respect for my life!"

The angel of the LORD said to Elijah, "Go down with him; do not be afraid of him." So Elijah got up and went down with him to the king.

He told the king, "This is what the LORD says: Is it because there is no God in Israel for you to consult that you have sent messengers to consult Baal-zebub, the god of Ekron? Because you have done this, you will never leave the bed you are lying on. You will certainly die!" So he died, according to the word of the LORD that Elijah had spoken.

Ahaziah thought he could avoid God's word by avoiding God's prophet. Now he thinks he can control God's word by controlling God's prophet. The problem is that controlling God's prophet is not easy! The army captains give the game away when they address Elijah as "Man of God". If Elijah is a man of God, then fifty troops will never be enough to capture him. The key phrase is: "according to the word of the LORD that Elijah had spoken" (1 v 17). Elijah spoke and Ahaziah died. Cause and effect. God's word is certain. God rules through His word. This is how His kingdom takes shape in the world, and human kings cannot resist His kingdom.

In contrast to these kings who challenged or avoided God's word, listen to the writer's assessment of Hezekiah:

2 Kings 18 v 3-6
[Hezekiah] did what was right in the eyes of the LORD, just as his father David had done. He removed the high places, smashed the sacred stones and cut down the Asherah poles. He broke into pieces the bronze snake Moses had made, for up to that time the Israelites had been burning incense to it. (It was called Nehushtan.)

Hezekiah trusted in the LORD, the God of Israel. There was no-one like him among all the kings of Judah, either before him or after him. He held fast to the LORD and did not cease to follow him; he kept the commands the LORD had given Moses.

Hezekiah is like David—the ultimate accolade given by the writer of the book of Kings. He not only removes the high places and sacred stones of Canaanite religion, he destroys the bronze snake—a part of Israel's heritage—because it was being venerated (Numbers 21 v 4-9). The key thing is that Hezekiah rules in obedience to the word of God.

In 1 and 2 Kings the warnings of Deuteronomy slowly unfold as the nation turns from God. The book of Deuteronomy promised blessings if the people were obedient, but it also outlined curses if they were not faithful to the covenant (see especially Deuteronomy 28 and 30). This is the principle by which the writer of Kings interprets history. What happens to Israel happens because those curses come into play. God's word is sovereign and so there is something inexorable about the story. The disaster that falls on Israel is a result of the judging and destroying power of God's law. God's word sets in train events that cannot be altered.

With the reign of King Manasseh the southern kingdom of Judah reaches the point of no return (2 Kings 21). Josiah slows the process down through his reforms, but he cannot prevent judgment coming (2 Kings 22 – 23). Once Israel had proved herself unfaithful to God, nothing could avert the curses of Deuteronomy falling.

Figure 26 shows how the different components of the promise were built up through the history of Israel, only to come crashing down with the defeat by Babylon. The book of Exodus is the story of God's people set free. The books of Joshua and Judges describe how God gives the people the promised land. 1 and 2 Samuel describe how God establishes His anointed king. 1 Kings describes how Solomon builds the temple in Jerusalem—the symbol of God's presence with His people. But the second half of 1 Kings and the book of

2 Kings describe how the people turn from God until at the end everything is in ruins. The people are in exile. The land has been defeated. The king is in captivity. The temple has been destroyed.

Figure 26: From Genesis to 2 Kings to Jesus

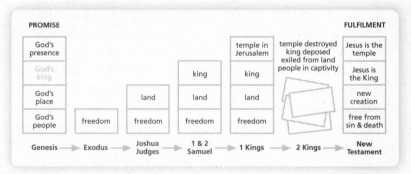

It seems as if the whole plan of salvation has run into the sand. All that is left is the bare promise. All that is left are the promises of God to Abraham, Moses and David. And so we get this strange anticlimax at the end of the story.

2 Kings 25 v 27-30

In the thirty-seventh year of the exile of Jehoiachin king of Judah, in the year Evil-Merodach became king of Babylon, he released Jehoiachin from prison on the twenty-seventh day of the twelfth month. He spoke kindly to him and gave him a seat of honour higher than those of the other kings who were with him in Babylon. So Jehoiachin put aside his prison clothes and for the rest of his life ate regularly at the king's table. Day by day the king gave Jehoiachin a regular allowance as long as he lived.

When we get to the end of the long history from Joshua

through to 2 Kings, we expect some gushing finale or some tragic final word. We would even settle for some kind of summary. But instead we get Jehoiachin receiving pocket money. Here at the end the covenant with David is still a brooding presence. It is not explicit, but it is there as a big hint. Maybe, just maybe, Jehoiachin will become God's anointed king. And if not Jehoiachin, then maybe one of his descendants. Maybe, while Jehoiachin is alive, there is hope.

It is worth asking why God took this route to achieve His purposes. Why do we get this arc of triumph and failure? Why did He not simply send Jesus after the promise to Abraham? The answer I think is to demonstrate for all eternity that salvation was not in any way achieved through human effort. God allowed the human institutions to come to nothing so that it would be forever clear that salvation was entirely by His power and grace. He did it so "that in the coming ages he might show the incomparable riches of his grace, expressed in his kindness to us in Christ Jesus" (Ephesians 2 v 7).

Prophecy: God will rule through a coming King

Out of the ruins of the kingdom the prophets bring a word of hope.

A coming kingdom

In a variety of ways God promises the coming of His reign. He promises to restore Israel and make her pre-eminent among the nations. He promises that He will come in judgment against Israel's enemies. He speaks of "a day of the LORD" in which evil will be judged and God's name will be vindicated.

A coming King

Alongside these promises of a new kingdom, God promises a new King. He will raise up a new David who will re-establish God's rule over His people. And He will rule not only over Israel, but over all nations.

Isaiah 9 v 6-7

For to us a child is born, to us a son is given, and the government will be on his shoulders. And he will be called Wonderful Counsellor, Mighty God, Everlasting Father, Prince of Peace. Of the increase of his government and peace there will be no end. He will reign on David's throne and over his kingdom, establishing and upholding it with justice and righteousness from that time on and for ever. The zeal of the LORD Almighty will accomplish this.

In Ezekiel 34 God denounces the shepherds—that is, the leaders—of Israel. Instead He promises to send a new David—the great Shepherd King—to gather His flock and reign over them:

Ezekiel 34 v 23-24

I will place over them one shepherd, my servant David, and he will tend them; he will tend them and be their shepherd. I the LORD will be their God, and my servant David will be prince among them. I the LORD have spoken.

Jesus: the promised Saviour-King

1. God's kingdom has come

In Mark 1 Jesus arrives on the scene, announcing the coming of God's kingdom and calling upon people to repent (1 v 15). Jesus is re-establishing God's rule. Matthew talks about "the kingdom of heaven", but this is simply an accommodation to the Jewish convention of avoiding the use of God's name.

2. God's King has come
Jesus is the son of David—the promised King. He is the Messiah. The kingdom has come because the King has come. Gabriel says to Mary:

> **Luke 1 v 31-33**
> "You will be with child and give birth to a son, and you are to give him the name Jesus. He will be great and will be called the Son of the Most High. The Lord God will give him the throne of his father David, and he will reign over the house of Jacob for ever; his kingdom will never end."

Jesus demonstrates His authority over people (Mark 1 v 16-20), in teaching (Mark 1 v 22), over evil spirits (Mark 1 v 23-27) and over sickness (Mark 1 v 29-34). He even claims authority to forgive sins (Mark 2 v 1-12). He exercises authority over the natural world (Mark 4 v 35-41) and over death (Mark 5 v 21-24, 35-43).

But there is a surprise. God's kingdom has come because God's King has come. But Jesus is also opposed and rejected. How can this be the coming of God's kingdom? This is not what we expected. We expected the kingdom of God to come in great glory, sweeping away God's enemies and vindicating His people (Matthew 3 v 10). So is this the real thing?

In response, Jesus tells a series of parables about the kingdom.

Matthew 13 v 31-33

He told them another parable: "The kingdom of heaven is like a mustard seed, which a man took and planted in his field. Though it is the smallest of all your seeds, yet when it grows, it is the largest of garden plants and becomes a tree, so that the birds of the air come and perch in its branches."

He told them still another parable: "The kingdom of heaven is like yeast that a woman took and mixed into a large amount of flour until it worked all through the dough."

At present the kingdom is small and hidden (see Matthew 13 v 11). But one day it will be like the largest of trees. It will be like yeast working throughout the entire dough. The reign of God is hidden now, but one day He will rule over everything.

Matthew 13 v 24-30

Jesus told them another parable: "The kingdom of heaven is like a man who sowed good seed in his field. But while everyone was sleeping, his enemy came and sowed weeds among the wheat, and went away. When the wheat sprouted and formed ears, then the weeds also appeared.

"The owner's servants came to him and said, 'Sir, didn't you sow good seed in your field? Where then did the weeds come from?'

"'An enemy did this,' he replied.

"The servants asked him, 'Do you want us to go and pull them up?'"

"'No,' he answered, 'because while you are pulling the weeds, you may root up the wheat with them. Let both grow together until the harvest. At that time I will tell the harvesters: First collect the weeds and tie them in bundles to be burned; then gather the wheat and bring it into my barn.'"

Matthew 13 v 36-43

Then he left the crowd and went into the house. His disciples came to him and said, "Explain to us the parable of the weeds in the field."

He answered, "The one who sowed the good seed is the Son of Man. The field is the world, and the good seed stands for the sons of the kingdom. The weeds are the sons of the evil one, and the enemy who sows them is the devil. The harvest is the end of the age, and the harvesters are angels.

"As the weeds are pulled up and burned in the fire, so it will be at the end of the age. The Son of Man will send out his angels, and they will weed out of his kingdom everything that causes sin and all who do evil. They will throw them into the fiery furnace, where there will be weeping and gnashing of teeth. Then the righteous will shine like the sun in the kingdom of their Father. He who has ears, let him hear."

Just because the kingdom has not come in glory and judgment does not mean it has not come. And just because it has come secretly does not mean it will not come in glory and judgment in the future.

In the meantime the kingdom grows as "the message about the kingdom" (13 v 19) is proclaimed and when a person "hears the word and understands it" (13 v 23). Once again, we see that God rules through His word, and extends His rule through His word.

Jewish expectations were right: the kingdom of God will come in great power and glory. But first it comes in a hidden, gracious way. Jesus is the Christ (God's anointed King), but He is the Christ who must suffer and die. Peter cannot accept this (Matthew 16 v 21-23). The Jewish leaders will not recognise this (Matthew 27 v 41-42). But Jesus says that this fulfils the Old Testament.

Luke 24 v 44-47

He said to them, "This is what I told you while I was still with you: Everything must be fulfilled that is written about me in the Law of Moses, the Prophets and the Psalms."

Then he opened their minds so they could understand the Scriptures. He told them, "This is what is written: The Christ will suffer and rise from the dead on the third day, and repentance and forgiveness of sins will be preached in his name to all nations, beginning at Jerusalem."

The Christ must suffer. After all, David the christ had suffered. So the early church turned to the Old Testament, especially the Psalms, to show that the Christ must suffer.

The Christ must suffer because it is by dying that He includes us in God's kingdom. If God had come first in power and judgment, none of us would stand (Malachi 3 v 1-5). But God comes first in judgment against His own Son. The King gives His life for His people. Jesus dies for His people so that they might experience His coming rule as blessing, life, peace and justice. And in so doing He redefines what rule means: "For even the Son of Man did not come to be served, but to serve, and to give his life as a ransom for many" (Mark 10 v 40-45).

If the death of Jesus redefines the nature of kingship, the resurrection of Jesus confirms that the crucified One is God's promised King. God has made Jesus Lord and King by raising him from the dead. This was the message of the apostles. They saw the Old Testament promise of a coming King fulfilled in the resurrection.

Acts 2 v 32, 36
God has raised this Jesus to life, and we are all witnesses of the fact … Therefore let all Israel be assured of this: God has made this Jesus, whom you crucified, both Lord and Christ.

Acts 13 v 32-33
We tell you the good news: What God promised our fathers he has fulfilled for us, their children, by raising up Jesus. As it is written in the second Psalm:

"You are my Son;
today I have become your Father."

The church: King Jesus rules through the gospel

Matthew 28 v 18-20
Then Jesus came to them and said, "All authority in heaven and on earth has been given to me. Therefore go and make disciples of all nations, baptising them in the name of the Father and of the Son and of the Holy Spirit, and teaching them to obey everything I have commanded you. And surely I am with you always, to the very end of the age."

It is because all authority has been given to Him that Jesus sends us to all the nations. It is through the preaching of the gospel that Jesus is wielding His sceptre in the world. Even now He exercises His rule through the preaching of the gospel. Through the gospel we command people to submit to Jesus. Through the gospel judgment is passed on people who continue to reject Him. To tell people the gospel is to announce the kingdom or kingship of God and His Christ.

We are ambassadors for Christ, bringing an authoritative pronouncement from the King. When we preach the gospel, we are heralds of a coming King. We go to the citizens of a country and say that a King is coming who rightly claims their allegiance. Those who currently rule them are usurpers and tyrants. If they acknowledge His lordship, they will experience His rule as blessing, life and salvation. If they reject Him, they will experience Him as their conqueror and judge.

- We do not invite people to make Jesus their King—we tell people that Jesus is the King and He will rule all of us for ever.
- We do not invite people to meet Jesus—we tell people that they will meet Jesus as their conquering King.
- We do not ask people to live better lives and make the world a better place—we command people to repent and submit to the coming King.

Of course, we do this graciously and gently (1 Peter 3 v 15-16). We cannot force or manipulate anyone to repent. But one day everyone will bow the knee before Jesus, whether they like it or not (Philippians 2 v 9-11).

If you want to defeat your enemy in battle, you surprise them. But God does not want to defeat us. And so He announces His coming. If you want to defeat your enemy, you make sure they have nowhere to escape. But God does not want to defeat us. And so He provides a way of escape. He "defeats" His own Son so that we can escape His coming in judgment.

New creation: God's everlasting rule of freedom

Revelation 5 v 1-5

Then I saw in the right hand of him who sat on the throne a scroll with writing on both sides and sealed with seven seals. And I saw a mighty angel proclaiming in a loud voice, "Who is worthy to break the seals and open the scroll?" But no-one in heaven or on earth or under the earth could open the scroll or even look inside it. I wept and wept because no-one was found who was worthy to open the scroll or look inside. Then one of the elders said to me, "Do not weep! See, the Lion of the tribe of Judah, the Root of David, has triumphed. He is able to open the scroll and its seven seals."

The scrolls in the book of Revelation represent the acts of history. The One worthy to open them is the One who controls history. Is there such a one? John, in his vision, fears not. But "then one of the elders said to me, 'Do not weep! See, the Lion of the tribe of Judah, the Root of David, has triumphed. He is able to open the scroll and its seven seals'"(Revelation 5 v 5). Yet when John sees the Davidic King, he sees "a Lamb, looking as if it had been slain" (Revelation 5 v 6). The elders and the living creatures sing: "You are worthy to take the scroll and to open its seals, because you were slain, and with your blood you purchased men for God from every tribe and language and people and nation" (Revelation 5 v 9).

When the seventh angel sounds his trumpet, loud voices in heaven say: "The kingdom of the world has become the kingdom of our Lord and of his Christ, and he will reign for ever and ever" (Revelation 11 v 15). In Revelation 21 – 22 we get a picture of life under the restored rule of God. It is life without threat, sin, pain, suffering or death. It is a life of blessing, abundance and security. It is a life of true freedom. The power of sin and death have been broken. We are free to be what we were intended to be—people who know and worship God. And that is good news.

Summary

Psalm 2 is written about the king of Israel. But it was never fulfilled in the Israelite kings. It points forward to David's greater Son. There are four sections, each with three verses. In each section there is a different speaker.

1. Mankind: We reject the rule of God and His anointed King (Psalm 2 v 1-3)

Why do the nations conspire and the peoples plot in vain? The kings of the earth take their stand and the rulers gather together against the LORD and against his Anointed One. "Let us break their chains," they say, "and throw off their fetters."

2. God: I will rule through my anointed King (v 4-6)

The One enthroned in heaven laughs; the LORD scoffs at them. Then he rebukes them in his anger and terrifies them in his wrath, saying, "I have installed my King on Zion, my holy hill."

3. God's King: God has made me King and I will rule the nations (v 7-9)

I will proclaim the decree of the LORD: He said to me, "You

are my Son; today I have become your Father. Ask of me,
and I will make the nations your inheritance, the ends of
the earth your possession. You will rule them with an iron
sceptre; you will dash them to pieces like pottery."

4. The people of God: "Submit to the coming King and find refuge in Him" (v 10-12)

Therefore, you kings, be wise; be warned, you rulers of the
earth. Serve the LORD with fear and rejoice with trembling.
Kiss the Son, lest he be angry and you be destroyed in your
way, for his wrath can flare up in a moment. Blessed are all
who take refuge in him.

This is a definition of the Kingdom of God. Humanity has
rejected the rule of God. But God remains sovereign. He
will re-establish His rule through His King. God's King is
coming to defeat and destroy those who reject His rule. But
He sends His people ahead to call on the nations to turn
to Him and find refuge. This is the Bible story. This is the
meaning of history. This is the gospel. This is the basis of
mission.

***

Case study: The promise of a King and the book of Nehemiah

How does the theme of God's promise of a King and a
kingdom help us understand the message of Nehemiah for
Christians today?

Nehemiah's description of his leadership (Nehemiah 5 v
14-19) seems consciously to echo Deuteronomy 17 v 14-20,
where the king is told not to use his power to accumulate

wealth. Nehemiah's leadership is also in contrast to the warnings of Samuel about Israel's king—warnings that proved all too true in the lives of so many of Israel's kings (1 Samuel 8; 12). Nehemiah not only organises the rebuilding of the wall, he is concerned that Israel live in obedience to God's word. Yet the book has the feel of an apologia or even a confession. His description of his leadership ends with a plea for God's favour (5 v 19).

Nehemiah 12 is the story of the celebration of the completed wall. It describes a great choir-fest with singing, the like of which had not been heard since David (12 v 27-28, 31, 38, 40, 43). Naturally in the story it should come after chapter 7 when the wall is rebuilt, but it has been held over to form a wonderful climax to the book. Except that this is not the end of the story. Chapter 12 is a premature celebration, a deliberate foil for the failings described in chapter 13. What is more, the events of chapter 13 actually come before those of chapter 12 (see 13 v 4). Nehemiah, or the editor, has placed this account of failure at the end of the book quite deliberately. The book has been carefully structured so that it ends in failure. The reforms of chapter 10 are all reversed in chapter 13. The book ends: "Remember me with favour, O my God" (13 v 31). It is a plea for grace.

Nehemiah is a great and godly leader. But ultimately he cannot give the people rest in the land (6 v 15 – 7 v 3). He cannot reform the people. He cannot give them the new exodus they need (9 v 36-37). He can liberate them from exile in Babylon, but he cannot rescue them from that to which the exile pointed—the power of sin and the judgment of God. Nehemiah is not so much a model for Christian leaders today as a pointer to the Lord Jesus Christ. To the extent that he partially fulfils the promise of God, he points to its full fulfilment in Christ. To the extent that he fails to fulfil the promise, he points to our need for a complete and sufficient Saviour and Leader.

Chapter 5

The promise of blessing to the nations

Figure 27: The promise of blessing to the nations

Creation	Commanded to fill the earth	
Fall	The nations against God	
Abraham	Promised blessing to all nations	
Israel	Called to draw the nations to God	
God's purposes	*Judgment to nations*	*Blessing to all nations*
God's people	*A threat from the nations*	*A light to the nations*
Into exile	Drawn to the ways of the nations	
Prophecy	Judgment and salvation to the nations	
Jesus	The hope of the nations	
The church	The gospel to all nations	
New creation	People from every nation	

There are over 200 countries in the world—a number that has grown in recent years. But countries are just entities defined by geographic boundaries. The biblical term "nation" has more the sense of ethnic group or people group—a group with a common cultural tradition and often a common language. There are 11,000 such people groups in the world today, 17,000 if you include people groups divided across geographic boundaries. Of those with more than 10,000 members (about half the total) 1,600 are unreached by the gospel (defined as having less than 2 per cent evangelical Christians). Furthermore, there are 7,148 languages in the world, of which 2,000 do not have a translation of the New Testament. Between 1.2 and 1.4 billion people have not heard the gospel. What are God's purposes for these nations?

Creation: commanded to fill the earth

When God made man and woman in His image we read: "God blessed them and said to them, 'Be fruitful and increase in number; fill the earth and subdue it'" (Genesis 1 v 28). They are to "increase in number" and they are to "fill the earth". There is a double process of multiplication and dispersion, which will lead to diversity. This is God's purpose for humanity. The process is interrupted by the flood at the time of Noah, but after the flood the command comes again: "As for you, be fruitful and increase in number; multiply on the earth and increase upon it" (Genesis 9 v 7).

In Genesis 10 we get what is called "the table of nations". It is an account of the sons of Noah "by their clans, their languages, their lands and their nations" (Genesis 10 v 5,20,31 ESV). It ends: "These are the clans of Noah's sons, according to their lines of descent, within their nations. From these the nations spread out over the earth after the flood" (Genesis 10 v 32). This is the diversity of nations that God intended.

Fall: The nations against God

In the book of Genesis, chapter 10 is placed prior to chapter 11 to bring out the contrast between God's intention and its corruption by human sin (even though Genesis 11 v 1 suggests the events of Genesis 11 may have preceded many of the developments of Genesis 10). Genesis 10 shows the diversity of nations that God intended, but in Genesis 11 the people of the world come together in opposition to God. The nations are part of God's purposes, but they are also opposed to God's purposes. These twin themes run throughout the Bible story.

Genesis 11 v 1-9

Now the whole world had one language and a common speech. As men moved eastward, they found a plain in Shinar and settled there.

They said to each other, "Come, let's make bricks and bake them thoroughly." They used brick instead of stone, and bitumen for mortar. Then they said, "Come, let us build ourselves a city, with a tower that reaches to the heavens, so that we may make a name for ourselves and not be scattered over the face of the whole earth."

But the LORD came down to see the city and the tower that the men were building. The LORD said, "If as one people speaking the same language they have begun to do this, then nothing they plan to do will be impossible for them. Come, let us go down and confuse their language so they will not understand each other."

So the LORD scattered them from there over all the earth, and they stopped building the city. That is why it was called Babel—because there the LORD confused the language of the whole world. From there the LORD scattered them over the face of the whole earth.

The people of the world come together on the plain of Shinar and say: "Come, let us build ourselves a city, with a tower that reaches to the heavens, so that we may make a name for ourselves and not be scattered over the face of the whole earth" (Genesis 11 v 4). This is the first proclamation of empire. The city and its tower were designed to keep people together rather than fulfilling God's command to spread out. It is an expression of human pride ("so that we may make a name for ourselves") and human rebellion against God ("and not be scattered over the face of the whole earth"). A characteristic of imperialism ever since has been its move towards ethnic and linguistic conformity.

But God prevents the formation of a single empire in opposition to Him, for it would become a cauldron of evil. "The LORD said, 'If as one people speaking the same language they have begun to do this, then nothing they plan to do will be impossible for them'" (Genesis 11 v 6). God sends different languages so that the people scatter "over the face of the whole earth" (Genesis 11 v 8, 9). The result is what He commanded in Genesis 1 and 9. Ethnic difference—and especially language, which is a key element of ethnic identity—is both a fulfilment of God's command and a judgment on our disobedience.

Abraham: promised blessing to all nations
It is in the context of God's purposes for the nations (Genesis

10) and God's judgment on the nations (Genesis 6 – 9; 11) that God makes His covenant with Abraham.

Genesis 12 v 3
"I will bless those who bless you, and whoever curses you I will curse; and all peoples on earth will be blessed through you."

Genesis 18 v 18
"Abraham will surely become a great and powerful nation, and all nations on earth will be blessed through him."

God changes Abraham's name from "Abram", which means "exalted father", to "Abraham", which means "father of a multitude":

Genesis 17 v 4-6
"As for me, this is my covenant with you: You will be the father of many nations. No longer will you be called Abram; your name will be Abraham, for I have made you a father of many nations. I will make you very fruitful; I will make nations of you, and kings will come from you."

The choice of Abraham is the point in the story where God focuses down on one person, one family and one nation. Prima facie, this is the point where God excludes the nations. But in fact, right from the beginning God says that His purposes for Abraham and Israel are for the sake of the nations.

When Paul wants to defend his mission to the Gentiles or nations, he does not turn to the Great Commission, though he might have done. He turns instead to the Old Testament and to the promise of God to Abraham:

Galatians 3 v 8, 29

The Scripture foresaw that God would justify the Gentiles [the nations] by faith, and announced the gospel in advance to Abraham: "All nations will be blessed through you" ... If you belong to Christ, then you are Abraham's seed, and heirs according to the promise.

The promise to Abraham of blessing to the nations is Paul's mandate for mission (see also Romans 1 v 1-6; 9 v 24-29; 16 v 25-27; Ephesians 3 v 1-6). It is also foundational to Paul's understanding of salvation. We are saved by faith without needing the signs of Jewish identity (sabbath, circumcision) because God's plan was always for blessing to extend beyond Jewish identity.

In Abraham's life we see him rescuing nations (Genesis 14) and interceding for nations (Genesis 18 v 22-33). But we also see him failing his calling. Shortly after the promise of blessing to the nations Abraham lies to the king of Egypt about Sarai (her name is later changed to Sarah) so that the king takes her into his household with the result that "the LORD inflicted serious diseases on Pharaoh and his household" (Genesis 12 v 17, see also Genesis 20). God has chosen Abraham to bless all nations, but Abraham will only do this as he directs his family in the ways of the LORD (Genesis 18 v 18-19).

Israel: drawing the nations to the rule of God

So far we have seen God both judging the nations and promising blessing to the nations. With the formation of Israel through the exodus and beyond, the calling of God's people—already there in Abraham (Genesis 18 v 18-19)—is clarified as Figure 28 shows.

Figure 28: God and the nations

	Judgment to the nations	Blessing to the nations
God's purposes and the nations	Judgment to the nations	Blessing to the nations
God's people and the nations	A threat from the nations	A light to the nations

A light to the nations

The Ten Commandments form the centrepiece of the law of Moses. There are two records of the Ten Commandments in the Old Testament (in Exodus 20 and Deuteronomy 5). Both accounts are introduced in a way that explains how the law was to define Israel's relationship to the nations.

> **Exodus 19 v 4-6**
> "'You yourselves have seen what I did to Egypt, and how I carried you on eagles' wings and brought you to myself. Now if you obey me fully and keep my covenant, then out of all nations you will be my treasured possession. Although the whole earth is mine, you will be for me a kingdom of priests and a holy nation.' These are the words you are to speak to the Israelites."

This is a key statement of God's purposes for Israel. It starts with God's initiative in redemption (19 v 4). Verse 5 is a strong statement of particularity: "out of all nations you will be my treasured possession". But even this is set in the context of God's universal claim on the nations ("the whole earth is mine"). Moreover the particularity of Israel is for a purpose: "you will be for me a kingdom of priests and a holy nation" (19 v 6). In Israel the priests taught the law and offered sacrifices of atonement so that the people could come to God. Here God calls on Israel to be a priestly kingdom in the midst of the nations. The nation as a whole is to take the knowledge of God to the nations and bring the nations to the means of atonement with God. "Holy" means "set apart". To be a holy nation was to be a distinctive nation among the nations. They were to be a nation that reflected the holiness of God and so made Him known to the nations. "Be holy because I, the LORD your God, am holy" (Leviticus 19 v 2). The law is given to this end. The law is missionary in intent. It defined what it meant for Israel to be a priestly kingdom and a holy nation that would make God known to the nations and bring the nations to God through atonement.

The second account of the Ten Commandments is introduced with these words:

Deuteronomy 4 v 5-8

See, I have taught you decrees and laws as the LORD my God commanded me, so that you may follow them in the land you are entering to take possession of it. Observe them carefully, for this will show your wisdom and understanding to the nations, who will hear about all these decrees and say, "Surely this great nation is a wise and understanding people." What other nation is so great as to have their gods near them the way the LORD our God is near us whenever we pray to him? And what other nation is so great as to have such righteous decrees and laws as this body of laws I am setting before you today?

Moses makes a big claim for the law of God. He claims that when it is compared with the legislation of other nations people will agree that it displays more wisdom and more righteousness. Israel is to model life under the rule of God through obedience to His word. In this way the nations will see that God's rule brings life and blessing. They will see what it is like to know God—to have Him "near" to you. Israel will commend God and His kingdom to the nations.

The inclusion of foreigners

The Israelites were not only to make God known to the nations, they were also to welcome people from other nations. "You are to love those who are aliens, for you yourselves were aliens in Egypt" (Deuteronomy 10 v 19). These immigrants had equal rights before the law. They were to be considered part of the community. Throughout its history Israel incorporated foreigners. Indeed the original people who escaped from Egypt were far from racially homogenous.

Of the four women mentioned in the genealogy of Matthew—a genealogy primarily designed to establish Jesus' Jewish credentials—three were Gentiles and the fourth may have been (Matthew 1 v 1-17). Tamar and Rahab were Canaanites (Genesis 38 and Joshua 2; 6). Ruth was a Moabite (Ruth 1 – 4). Bathsheba is not referred to by name, but as "Uriah's wife" (2 Samuel 11). This may be to emphasise that Uriah was a Hittite and, although she may have been an Israelite, after her marriage Bathsheba would have been regarded as a Hittite. Therefore woven into the genealogy of the King of Israel are four Gentile women.

A threat from the nations

The nations are objects of God's grace expressed through the witness of His people. But the nations and their gods are also seen as a threat to the people of God. When Joshua takes the land of Canaan, he is to destroy everyone and everything belonging to the Canaanite nations.

When Achan keeps some of the spoils of war, the whole community is punished (Joshua 7). Everything is said to be "devoted... to destruction" (Joshua 6 v 21 ESV). This is an act of judgment against those nations. God delayed giving the land to Abraham's family because "the sin of the Amorites has not yet reached its full measure" (Genesis 15 v 16). It prefigures the final day of judgment. But devotion of everything to destruction is also to protect God's people from the influence of the nations.

After Joshua dies, the people compromise this command for purity. Instead of driving out the nations, they follow their ways. God judges His people by handing them over to their enemies, until they cry out to Him and He raises up judges to free them. But they do not learn their lesson. So in judgment God gives them what they want.

> **Judges 2 v 21-22**
> "I will no longer drive out before them any of the nations Joshua left when he died. I will use them to test Israel and see whether they will keep the way of the LORD and walk in it as their forefathers did."

Now each new generation will face conflict with the nations that will test its fidelity to God (Judges 3 v 1-2). God's people will either be a light to the nations or they will be corrupted by the nations.

Throughout history the people of God—first Israel and then the church—are in conflict with the world around them. The people of the world divide into two groups—sometimes thought of as two humanities or two cities. Humanity in opposition to God persecutes the people of God. It is Egypt, then Canaan, then Philistia, then Assyria, then Babylon and then Rome. Sometimes it is presented in mythical terms, as in Ezekiel's vision of Gog and Magog (Ezekiel 38 – 39). The most common expression of this conflict is the contrast between Babylon and Jerusalem, which the Apostle John picks up in the book of Revelation. Babel becomes Babylon—the symbol of humanity in opposition to God and His people.

Decline into exile: drawn to the ways of the nations

In the reign of Solomon Israel reaches it zenith as a light to the nations, but the seeds of its failure are also sown. Under Solomon Israel attracts the nations. The queen of Sheba travels from the ends of the world to hear God's wisdom from Solomon (1 Kings 10 v 1-13). The nations bring their wealth to enrich God's people and God's temple (1 Kings 10 v 14-29). This is as good as the fulfilment of Deuteronomy 4 v 5-8 gets in the Old Testament: "Men of all nations came to listen to Solomon's wisdom, sent by all the kings of the world, who had heard of his wisdom" (1 Kings 4 v 34). But Solomon also marries foreign wives who bring their foreign gods (1 Kings 11 v 1-3). Solomon himself joins in their worship (1 Kings 11 v 4-8). The call to be a light to the nations and the threat from the nations are both there in his reign.

The writer of Kings assesses the nation of Israel and her kings in accordance with the calling to be a light to the nations. The LORD drove out the wicked nations of Canaan so that there might be a place on earth where the goodness of life under His rule could be seen by the nations. The tragedy of Israel is that it reverted to the ways of those wicked nations. "The people engaged in all the detestable practices of the nations the LORD had driven out before the Israelites" (1 Kings 14 v 24; see also 2 Kings 16 v 3; 17 v 8,11,15,33; 21 v 2). Far from bringing their glory into God's kingdom, the nations now corrupt God's people, attack Jerusalem and plunder the temple. The contrast between Solomon's reign and Rehoboam's reign is stark:

Figure 29: Solomon's reign and Rehoboam's reign

Solomon's reign	Rehoboam's reign
God's people are a light to the nations	God's people follow the ways of the nations (1 Kings 14 v 24)
The nations come to Jerusalem to marvel	The nations come to Jerusalem to attack (1 Kings 14 v 25)
The nations bring their glory to Jerusalem	The nations plunder the glory of Jerusalem (1 Kings 14 v 26)
Solomon builds a glorious temple with golden treasures	Rehoboam makes bronze items for the temple (1 Kings 14 v 27-28)

The nation reaches the point of no return under the reign of Manasseh. The people do not listen to the word of God (2 Kings 21 v 7-9a). Instead "Manasseh led them astray, so that they did more evil than the nations the Lord had destroyed before the Israelites" (2 Kings 21 v 9b). They are no longer a light to the nations. They do not even follow the ways of the nations. They are actually *more* evil than the nations.

Because Israel turns from God and His word to follow the ways of the nations, God uses the nations to judge them. Defeat at the hand of the nations is portrayed as the judgment of God. 2 Kings 17 describes the end of the northern kingdom of Israel. The people are defeated by the Assyrians, carried away into exile and lost to history for ever. But the writer portrays it all as the judgment of God upon them because they followed the ways of the nations and would not turn back to God and His word. In the same way Jeremiah says that God will use Babylon to bring judgment on the southern kingdom of Judah. God even calls the king of Babylon "my servant":

Jeremiah 25 v 9
"I will summon all the peoples of the north and my servant Nebuchadnezzar king of Babylon," declares the LORD, "and I will bring them against this land and its inhabitants and against all the surrounding nations. I will completely destroy them and make them an object of horror and scorn, and an everlasting ruin" (See also Jeremiah 27 v 6; 43 v 10.)

Prophecy: Judgment and salvation will come to the nations

Judgment to the nations

When the Babylonians defeated Judah for the first time, they took away some of the Jerusalem elite, including Daniel and Ezekiel. Ezekiel ministered to the exiles in Babylon. Ezekiel 4 – 24 contains Ezekiel's warning of judgment to God's people—Jerusalem and the temple will be destroyed. He has two repeated refrains: "Then they will know that I am the LORD" and "I am against you". In chapters 25 – 32 Ezekiel addresses the surrounding nations. He moves anti-clockwise around Israel: Ammon (25 v 6-7), Moab (25 v 10-11), Edom (25 v 12-14), Philistia (25 v 15-17), Tyre (26 v 1-6), Sidon (28 v 21-24), Egypt (29 v 3-6). The same two refrains are repeated throughout this section. The message to the nations is the same message as the message to Israel.

Do not misunderstand Israel's downfall: Israel's God is your God

The nations are not to suppose that their triumph over Israel means their gods are more powerful. The nations are told: "You will know that I am the LORD" (Ezekiel 25 v 5, 7, 11, 17; 26 v 6; 28 v 22, 23, 24; 28 v 26; 29 v 6, 9, 16, 21; 30 v 8, 19, 25, 26; 32 v 15). God addresses the nations because He is the God of all the earth. He has a moving throne because His sovereignty is not limited to one geographic location (Ezekiel 1 v 1, 3, 15-28).

Do not delight in Israel's downfall: Israel's fate will be your fate

The nations are also told: "I am against you" (Ezekiel 26 v 3; 28 v 22; 29 v 3, 10; 30 v 22). The exile in Babylon is a picture of humanity's fate—we will all be defeated by God and eternally exiled from the blessing and peace of His loving reign.

This is Ezekiel's theology of mission. Israel should have been a light and blessing to the nations. Instead Israel profaned God's holy name before the nations. But where Israel fails, God Himself will act.

Ezekiel 36 v 22-33

"Therefore say to the house of Israel, 'This is what the Sovereign LORD says: It is not for your sake, O house of Israel, that I am going to do these things, but for the sake of my holy name, which you have profaned among the nations where you have gone. I will show the holiness of my great name, which has been profaned among the nations, the name you have profaned among them. Then the nations will know that I am the LORD, declares the Sovereign LORD, when I show myself holy through you before their eyes.'"

Salvation to the nations

The prophets tell us that the new thing that God is going to do for Israel will encompass the nations (Isaiah 11 v 10-16; 19 v 18-25). "Many nations," says God, "will become my people" (Zechariah 2 v 11). God will gather His people scattered in exile, but at the same time He will gather people from the four corners of the world (Isaiah 56 v 6-8; 66 v 18-21). The song of God's praise will go into all the earth (Isaiah 12 v 5-6). The Apostle James quotes from Amos 9 v 11-12 at the Council of Jerusalem to argue that Gentiles can be part of the church without needing to be circumcised: "I will return and rebuild David's fallen tent ... that the remnant of men may seek the Lord, and all the Gentiles [the nations] who bear my name" (Acts 15 v 16-17). Israel had failed to model life under the rule of God in a way that attracted the nations, but the prophets promise that one day the nations will be drawn to God (Isaiah 2 v 1-5; Micah 4 v 1-5).

In Jonah we have the story of a Gentile nation that repents in response to the preaching of God's word. Jonah runs from God's commission to go to Nineveh not because he is afraid, but because he knows God to be gracious (see 2 Kings 14 v 23-27). He suspects that God will save Nineveh and Jonah does not want grace to extend to the nations (Jonah 4 v 2). But in the waters of the ocean Jonah experiences something of the godforsakenness of the nations and in that experience rediscovers the grace of God.

Jonah 2 v 2, 8-9
From the depths of the grave I called for help and you listened to my cry ... Those who cling to worthless idols forfeit the grace that could be theirs. But I, with a song of thanksgiving, will sacrifice to you. What I have vowed I will make good. Salvation comes from the LORD.

Jonah learns a new compassion for the nations that takes him to Nineveh (even if that compassion is short lived). Moreover, Jonah belongs among the prophets because his autobiography functions as a prophetic call to Israel to take up her responsibility to make the compassion of God known to the nations.

Isaiah has four songs about an unidentified "servant of the LORD" (Isaiah 42 v 1-9; 49 v 1-7; 50 v 4-9; 52 v 13 – 53 v 12). Sometimes these appear to be about Israel collectively, sometimes about an individual who brings salvation to Israel. They point to Jesus, who fulfils the calling of Israel, saves God's people through His suffering and brings justice to the nations (Isaiah 42 v 1, 4). Israel was to be a light to the nations, but she rarely lived up to this calling. Too often, instead of attracting the nations to God, she was attracted to the nations and their gods. But this calling to be a light to the nations will be fulfilled by the promised servant:

Isaiah 42 v 6
"I will keep you and will make you to be a covenant for the people and a light for the Gentiles [nations]…"

Isaiah 49 v 6
"I will also make you a light for the Gentiles [nations], that you may bring my salvation to the ends of the earth."

Jesus: the hope of the nations

With the promise of the servant still ringing in our ears, we hear Jesus say: "I am the light of the world" (John 8 v 12; see also John 1 v 4-9; 3 v 19-21; 9 v 5; 12 v 46; Acts 13 v 47). Jesus is the servant of the LORD promised by Isaiah and "in his name the nations will put their hope" (Matthew 12 v 15-21). Jesus is the one who brings good news to the nations.

He will gather faithful Israel, but He will also gather people from the four corners of the world (Mark 13 v 27). He is the one who fulfils Israel's calling to make God known to the nations. The nation of Israel has the priority in His earthly ministry (Matthew 10 v 5-6; 15 v 21-28), but as the nation and its leaders reject Him, so Israel loses its priority status (Matthew 21 v 33-46). Now the gospel goes to all those who will receive the good news, whether Jew or Gentile.

Luke begins his account of Jesus' ministry with a sermon at Nazareth, which defines His ministry. Jesus reads from Isaiah 61 v 1-2 and claims that it is fulfilled in Himself. In response "all spoke well of Him and were amazed at the gracious words that came from his lips" (Luke 4 v 22). But then Jesus predicts (or precipitates) their rejection of Him by highlighting the way that Elijah only fed a Gentile widow and Elisha only healed a Gentile soldier (4 v 24-27). The people welcomed the news of the promised salvation, but they are "furious" at the suggestion that salvation might come to other nations ahead of the Jewish nation (4 v 28-30). Then in Luke 7 Jesus heals the servant of a Gentile soldier (just as Elisha healed a Gentile soldier) and raises the son of a Gentile widow (as Elijah did), enacting that of which he had spoken in 4 v 24-27. In Luke 11 v 27-32 Jesus says that the Queen of the South and the people of Nineveh—both Gentiles—will condemn this generation because they—the Gentiles—responded to God's word. The salvation that Jesus brings will include people from all nations. "People will come from east and west and north and south, and will take their places at the feast in the kingdom of God" (Luke 13 v 29).

The Church: the gospel to the nations

The gospel to the world
Matthew 28 v 18-20
Then Jesus came to them and said, "All authority in heaven
and on earth has been given to me. Therefore go and make
disciples of all nations, baptising them in the name of the
Father and of the Son and of the Holy Spirit, and teaching
them to obey everything I have commanded you. And surely
I am with you always, to the very end of the age."

In the Old Testament the basic movement of mission was
to draw the nations to Jerusalem and the temple (Isaiah 2
v 1-5; Micah 4 v 1-5). The Great Commission reverses this
movement. Now the people of God are sent out into the
world (John 17 v 18).

Acts 1 v 8
"But you will receive power when the Holy Spirit comes on
you; and you will be my witnesses in Jerusalem, and in all
Judea and Samaria, and to the ends of the earth."

In Isaiah God said of His people: "You are my witnesses"
(Isaiah 43 v 10, 12). Now Jesus tells His disciples that they
will be His witnesses to the ends of the earth. At Pentecost
the gospel is proclaimed to people from many nations who
hear it in their own languages. Through the Holy Spirit
the confusion of Babel is reversed. The book of Acts is the
story of how the gospel moves from Jerusalem to Judea and
Samaria, and ultimately to Rome, at the centre of the then
known world. As Israel should have been, and as Jesus was,
the disciples are to be a light in a dark world (Matthew 5 v
14-16; Philippians 2 v 15; 1 Peter 2 v 12).

In Exodus 19 God outlined His purpose for His people in relation to the nations. In 1 Peter 2 v 9 Peter picks up the language of Exodus 19 and applies it to the church: The church is now the people of God and its purpose is the same as that set out in Exodus 19:

1 Peter 2 v 9, 12
that you may declare the praises of him who called you out of darkness into his wonderful light ... Live such good lives among the pagans that, though they accuse you of doing wrong, they may see your good deeds and glorify God on the day he visits us.

Figure 30: 1 Peter 2 and Exodus 19

1 Peter 2:9	Exodus 19:5-6
A chosen people	"My people, my chosen ... that they may proclaim my praise" (Isaiah 43 v 20-21)
A royal priesthood	A kingdom of priests
A holy nation	A holy nation
His own possession (ESV)	My treasured possession

Paul, too, speaks of "proclaiming the gospel" to the Gentiles (nations) as a "priestly duty" (Romans 15 v 16).

Writing to Timothy, Paul describes the church as "God's household ... the church of the living God, the pillar and foundation of the truth" (1 Timothy 3 v 15). The church upholds the truth of God in the world and Paul goes on to define that truth for us:

1 Timothy 3 v 16

Beyond all question, the mystery of godliness is great: He appeared in a body, was vindicated by the Spirit, was seen by angels, was preached among the nations, was believed on in the world, was taken up in glory.

It is part of the content of the truth that Christ is proclaimed to the nations and believed on in the world.

The threat from the world

Israel was to be a light to the nations, but they were also warned of the threat from the nations. It is the same for the church. Not only do we take the gospel to the world, we are warned of the corrupting influence of the world. The term "world"—especially in the writings of John—is used in two ways:

- The object of God's love and our mission (John 1 v 29; 3 v 16-17; 6 v 33; 12 v 47; 17 v 18, 21, 23; 1 John 2 v 2; 4 v 9, 14)
- Humanity in opposition to God and his people (John 7 v 7; 12 v 31; 15 v 18-19; 17 v 13-16; 1 John 2 v 15-17; 3 v 1, 13; 4 v 1-5; 5 v 4-5, 19)

This is why John can write "God so loved the world that he gave his one and only Son" (John 3 v 16) but also say: "Do not love the world or anything in the world. If anyone loves the world, the love of the Father is not in him" (1 John 2 v 15; see also Romans 12 v 2). The world lies in the power of the evil one (1 John 5 v 19). "The ways of this world" (Ephesians 2 v 2) are contrary to God and provoke His wrath. It was from this that we were saved, but the world continues to threaten and seduce Christians.

In John 17 v 11-19 Jesus prays for His disciples as He

leaves them in a hostile world. He prays that they might be kept by the word and sanctified by the truth. The disciples are not to be taken out of the world (17 v 15), but sent into the world (17 v 18). They will continue Jesus' mission of love as they proclaim His name. But they can only do this if they retain their distinctiveness from the world ("sanctified" means "set apart"). We are a light to the world when, and only when, we are different from the world.

New creation: people from every nation

Judgment to the nations

In the book of Revelation the conflict between Babylon and Jerusalem, between the world in opposition to God and God's people, that has gone on throughout history comes to a climax. We read of the persecution of God's faithful people (Revelation 13 v 5-10), who are warned not to be corrupted by Babylon (Revelation 18 v 4-5). But ultimately, Christ rides out to conquer the nations (Revelation 19 v 11-21, see also 12 v 5). This fulfils the promise that the king of the line of David would rule the nations (Psalm 2 v 9; Revelation 19 v 15). Babylon is finally defeated (Revelation 14 v 8; 18 v 2-3).

Salvation to the nations

The book of Revelation closes with a vision of a restored Eden, with a tree of life fed by the water that flows from the throne of the Lamb. "The leaves of the tree," we discover, "are for the healing of the nations" (Revelation 22 v 2). All the nations will come to worship God (Revelation 15 v 3-4).

A characteristic of imperialism ever since Babel has been its move towards ethnic and linguistic homogeneity. But the "empire" of the Lamb is different. It celebrates diversity.

Revelation 7 v 9-10

After this I looked and there before me was a great multitude that no-one could count, from every nation, tribe, people and language, standing before the throne and in front of the Lamb. They were wearing white robes and were holding palm branches in their hands. And they cried out in a loud voice: "Salvation belongs to our God, who sits on the throne, and to the Lamb."

Not only are representatives from every nation in the new creation, but they bring the best of their culture to enrich it. "The nations will walk by its light, and the kings of the earth will bring their splendour into it ... The glory and honour of the nations will be brought into it" (Revelation 21 v 24, 26).

"All peoples on earth will be blessed through you" said God to Abraham (Genesis 12 v 3). Now people from every nation are part of the new humanity in the new creation, enjoying God's rule of freedom, and nationality and culture are redeemed and enriched in the new Jerusalem.

***

Case study: the promise of a blessing to the nations and the book of Nehemiah

How does the theme of God's purposes for the nations help us understand the message of Nehemiah for Christians today?

In 5 v 1-13 we find that during a time of famine the poor have been forced to borrow from the rich, and some of the rich are using the situation to enslave the poor. Nehemiah is "very angry" when he hears this. Nehemiah had redeemed "brothers" from the nations. Now the rich are selling them into slavery again. Nehemiah says: "What you are doing is not right. Shouldn't you walk in the fear of our God to avoid the reproach of our Gentile enemies?" (5 v 9). In Nehemiah 6 v 15-16 the nations recognise that the wall has been built "with the help of our God". By redeeming slaves, God's people had witnessed to the liberating rule of God. But now this positive witness is threatened. The nations will associate God's rule with bondage and oppression. The same issues face us today. Christians are to reflect our experience of grace in the way we treat one another, so that people will see in us an illustration of the gospel (John 13 v 34-35).

In Nehemiah 6 v 1-14 the nations conspire against God's people. It is yet another example of a long history, which will come to a climax in the death of Christ and continue with the persecution of the church (Acts 4 v 23-31). The threat comes in more subtle forms as well. In 13 v 23-27 Nehemiah rebukes the people for allowing mixed marriages.

Nehemiah 13 v 26

"Was it not because of marriages like these that Solomon king of Israel sinned? Among the many nations there was no king like him. He was loved by his God, and God made him king over all Israel, but even he was led into sin by foreign women."

Even Solomon, the greatest king of his day, loved by God and blessed by God, was led astray by foreign influences. With such examples we can warn each other (1 Corinthians 10 v 11-13). Flirting with the world is deadly.

In 5 v 17 Nehemiah talks about "those who came to us from the surrounding nations" (Nehemiah 5 v 17). God's people today are to be an inclusive people, as they were in Nehemiah's day, for God's purposes embrace all peoples and groups.

Blessing and curse

The book of Deuteronomy ends with a terrible sense of foreboding. As the people stand on the verge of the promised land, Moses reminds them of God's gracious redemption and His liberating law. He then outlines the blessings that will come from following this law and the curses that will fall on the people if they forsake the law.

Deuteronomy 28 v 58-68
If you do not carefully follow all the words of this law, which are written in this book, and do not revere this glorious and awesome name—the LORD your God—the LORD will send fearful plagues on you and your descendants, harsh and prolonged disasters, and severe and lingering illnesses. He will bring upon you all the diseases of Egypt that you dreaded, and they will cling to you. The LORD will also bring on you every kind of sickness and disaster not recorded in this Book of the Law, until you are destroyed. You who were as numerous as the stars in the sky will be left but few in number, because you did not obey the LORD your God. Just as it pleased the LORD to make you prosper and increase in number, so it will please him to ruin and destroy you. You will be uprooted from the land you are entering to possess.

Then the LORD will scatter you among all nations, from one end of the earth to the other. There you will worship other gods—gods of wood and stone, which neither you nor your fathers have known. Among those nations you will find no repose, no resting place for the sole of your foot. There the LORD will give you an anxious mind, eyes weary with longing, and a despairing heart. You will live in constant suspense, filled with dread both night and day, never sure of your life. In the morning you will say, "If only it were evening!" and in the evening, "If only it were morning!"— because of the terror that will fill your hearts and the sights that your eyes will see. The LORD will send you back in ships to Egypt on a journey I said you should never make again. There you will offer yourselves for sale to your enemies as male and female slaves, but no-one will buy you.

It makes for grim reading. The plagues that fell in judgment on Egypt will fall now on God's own people. God had promised Abraham blessing in place of the curse that had fallen on humanity as a result of the fall. But if the people do not keep the covenant, the promise of Abraham will go into reverse. Instead of being as numerous as the stars, they will be few in number (28 v 62). Instead of knowing God, they will worship false gods (28 v 64). Instead of rest in the land of promise, they will be scattered among the nations without rest (28 v 64-65). Instead of redemption from Egypt, they will become slaves again in Egypt (28 v 68). The description of the curses that will befall the people are terrible:

Deuteronomy 28 v 53-55
Because of the suffering that your enemy will inflict on you during the siege, you will eat the fruit of the womb, the flesh of the sons and daughters the LORD your God has given you.

Even the most gentle and sensitive man among you will
have no compassion on his own brother or the wife he loves
or his surviving children, and he will not give to one of them
any of the flesh of his children that he is eating. It will be
all he has left because of the suffering that your enemy will
inflict on you during the siege of all your cities.

This is God's judgment spelt out for us in picture language.
It is a description of hell. This is our future. For what makes
the curses of Deuteronomy so poignant is that God predicts
that Israel will break the covenant.

Deuteronomy 31 v 16
And the LORD said to Moses: "You are going to rest with your
fathers, and these people will soon prostitute themselves
to the foreign gods of the land they are entering. They will
forsake me and break the covenant I made with them."

Yet the promise to Abraham still stands and it is a promise
without conditions. God *will* bless all nations through
Abraham and his descendants. The terms of the covenant
of Moses stand in tension with the promise to Abraham.
One predicts curses, the other promises blessing.

A clue to how this tension might be resolved is found
in the song of Moses that follows his prediction of Israel's
rebellion. The dominant image for God in the song is that
of a rock (Deuteronomy 32 v 4, 15,18, 30-31).

Deuteronomy 32 v 3-4
I will proclaim the name of the LORD. Oh, praise the
greatness of our God! He is the Rock, his works are perfect,
and all his ways are just. A faithful God who does no wrong,
upright and just is he.

This reflects a formative moment in the experience of Moses. Shortly after Moses had led the people out of Egypt, they grumbled against Moses and tested God. Moses called the place *Massah* and *Meribah*, which means "quarrelling" and "testing". He cried out in despair, "What I am to do with these people?" (Exodus 17 v 4).

Exodus 17 v 5-6
The LORD answered Moses, "Walk on ahead of the people. Take with you some of the elders of Israel and take in your hand the staff with which you struck the Nile, and go. I will stand there before you by the rock at Horeb. Strike the rock, and water will come out of it for the people to drink."

The rod that struck the Nile did so in judgment against Egypt. Now Moses is publicly to use that rod to strike the rock. Once again it is being wielded in judgment. But the judgment does not fall on the people as they deserve. Instead God takes the judgment on Himself. As a result water gushes out to bless the people. God takes judgment on Himself so that He might graciously bless His people.

And so it is in the image of God as a rock that Moses finds hope. The people of Israel will break the covenant. The song of Moses is clear about that: "You deserted the Rock, who fathered you; you forgot the God who gave you birth" (Deuteronomy 32 v 18). But if God could take judgment on Himself to bless His people at Massah and Meribah, then He could do it again.

And Moses was right. "[Our forefathers]," says Paul, "drank from the spiritual rock that accompanied them, and that rock was Christ" (1 Corinthians 10 v 4). The rock of Massah and Meribah was a picture of what Christ would do.

On the cross Christ took God's judgment on Himself so that He might bless His people. And so Jesus can say:

John 7 v 37-39
"If anyone is thirsty, let him come to me and drink. Whoever believes in me, as the Scripture has said, streams of living water will flow from within him." By this he meant the Spirit, whom those who believed in him were later to receive.

Just as the rock provided physical water to thirsty Israelites, so, through His death as our substitute, Jesus provides spiritual water to the spiritually thirsty (see also John 4 v 14).

In Luke 7 Jesus says:

Luke 7 v 33-35
"For John the Baptist came neither eating bread nor drinking wine, and you say, 'He has a demon.' The Son of Man came eating and drinking, and you say, 'Here is a glutton and a drunkard, a friend of tax collectors and "sinners".' But wisdom is proved right by all her children."

John the Baptist has sent his disciples to ask Jesus whether He is truly the Christ. When John's messengers have left, Jesus talks about the role of John the Baptist.

Luke tells us that, while many people had been baptised by John, the religious leaders had rejected his ministry. They could not be pleased. John came not eating and drinking and they rejected him. Jesus came eating and drinking—a sign that God's great eternal banquet was breaking into history (Luke 14 v 15-24)—and they called Him "a glutton and a drunkard". It is an allusion to Deuteronomy 21:

Deuteronomy 21 v 18-21

If a man has a stubborn and rebellious son who does not obey his father and mother and will not listen to them when they discipline him, his father and mother shall take hold of him and bring him to the elders at the gate of his town. They shall say to the elders, "This son of ours is stubborn and rebellious. He will not obey us. He is a profligate and a drunkard." Then all the men of his town shall stone him to death. You must purge the evil from among you. All Israel will hear of it and be afraid.

Jesus is, according to the religious leaders, "a profligate and a drunkard". In others words, He is a rebellious son of Israel who deserves to be executed. There is a double irony here. First, Jesus is in fact the faithful Son of Israel, while the Pharisees are the rebellious ones. Jesus says: "But wisdom is proved right by all her children" (Luke 7 v 35). In other words: "we will see who is the faithful child". God makes the new covenant with Jesus, the faithful One, who fulfils God's will perfectly so that those united to Christ by faith are counted faithful members of the covenant community. The second element of irony, however, is that Jesus did indeed die the death of a rebellious son of Israel. But He did not die for His own rebellion, but for the rebellion of His people. The next verses in Deuteronomy 21 are:

Deuteronomy 21 v 22-23

If a man guilty of a capital offence is put to death and his body is hung on a tree, you must not leave his body on the tree overnight. Be sure to bury him that same day, because anyone who is hung on a tree is under God's curse. You must not desecrate the land the LORD your God is giving you as an inheritance.

Paul quotes these words in Galatians 3:

Galatians 3 v 13-14
Christ redeemed us from the curse of the law by becoming
a curse for us, for it is written: "Cursed is everyone who is
hung on a tree." He redeemed us in order that the blessing
given to Abraham might come to the Gentiles through
Christ Jesus, so that by faith we might receive the promise of
the Spirit.

Paul is quoting Deuteronomy 21 v 23. Jesus bears the curses
of Deuteronomy. Jesus is the faithful Son, who dies the death
of a rebellious son. He is the King from God, who endures the
curses of those who reject God's rule. Jesus took on Himself
the curse in the form of the negation of every element of
the promise to Abraham. God promised Abraham a people
who knew God, but on the cross Jesus cries out: "My God,
my God, why have you forsaken me?" (Matthew 27 v 46)
In the promised land of blessing there is darkness (Matthew
27 v 45). The promised King wears a crown of thorns and
hangs under a sign proclaiming that this pathetic, dying
figure is the king of the Jews (Matthew 27 v 28-29, 37). This
is the hour in which the forces of darkness reign (Luke 22 v
53). The nations bring their plotting against the Lord and
His anointed to its terrible climax as they kill their Creator
(Acts 4 v 25-27).

Jesus takes the curse, losing everything that was promised
to Abraham and everything that was good in Eden. But he
takes the curse in our place so that those who put their faith
in Him need not fear it. If we rely on our own goodness,
then we will be cursed because none of us can keep the
whole law any more than the people of Israel could. "All
who rely on observing the law are under a curse," says

Paul, "for it is written: 'Cursed is everyone who does not continue to do everything written in the Book of the Law'" (Galatians 3 v 10).

But we can escape the terrible curses described in Deuteronomy through faith in the death of Jesus (Galatians 3 v 11). And not only do we escape the curses, but we also receive the blessings promised to Abraham. "He redeemed us in order that the blessing given to Abraham might come to the Gentiles [nations] through Christ Jesus, so that by faith we might receive the promise of the Spirit" (Galatians 3 v 14). Through faith in the cross the curse is lifted.

Now, as the gospel is proclaimed, God's ancient promise to bring blessing to all nations is being fulfilled. "The Scripture foresaw that God would justify the Gentiles [nations] by faith, and announced the gospel in advance to Abraham: 'All nations will be blessed through you'" (Galatians 3 v 8).

Further reading

Alexander, T. D. and **Rosner, Brian S.** (eds), *New Dictionary of Biblical Theology* (IVP, 2000).

Bartholomew, Craig and Michael Goheen, *The Drama of Scripture: Finding our Place in the Biblical Story* (Baker/SPCK, 2004/2006)'.

Bright, John, *The Kingdom of God* (Abingdon, 1953, 1981).

Goldsworthy, Graeme, *According to Plan: The Unfolding Revelation of God in the Bible* (IVP, 1991).

Goldsworthy, Graeme, *Gospel and Kingdom: A Christian Interpretation of the Old Testament* (Paternoster, 1981), also available in *The Goldsworthy Trilogy: Gospel and Kingdom, Gospel and Wisdom, The Gospel in Revelation* (Paternoster, 2000).

Martins, E. A., *Plot and Purpose in the Old Testament* (IVP, 1981).

Motyer, Alec, *Look to the Rock: An Old Testament Background to our Understanding of Christ* (IVP, 1996).

Roberts, Vaughan, *God's Big Picture* (IVP, 2003).

Strom, Mark, *Days are Coming: Exploring Biblical Patterns* (Hodder & Stoughton, 1989).

Van Gemeren, Willem, *The Progress of Redemption: From Creation to the New Jerusalem* (Paternoster, 1988).

Wright, Chris, *Knowing Jesus Through the Old Testament: Rediscovering the Roots of our Faith* (IVP, 1992).

Wright, Chris, *Living as the People of God: The Relevance of Old Testament Ethics* (IVP, 1983).

Wright, Chris, *The Mission of God: Unlocking the Bible's Grand Narrative* (IVP, 2006)'.

Also by Tim Chester

Gospel Centred Series

This series of accessible study guides aims to show how our churches, lives, families and leadership should be shaped by the priorities of the Gospel.

• **Gospel centred Church** with *Steve Timmis*

• **Gospel centred Family** with *Ed Moll*

• **Gospel Centred Life**

Good Book Guides

A wide range of excellent Bible-study guides suitable for individuals or small groups, covering the Old and New Testaments, and many topical issues. Tim is the series editor, and has also written a number of individual titles, including:

• **The Apostles Creed**

• **Experiencing God**

• **Ruth:** *Poverty and Plenty*

• **Psalms:** *Soul Songs*

• **Psalms:** *Work Songs*

• **Zechariah:** *God's Big Plan for Struggling Christians*

• **Ezekiel:** *God of Glory*

• **Mark 1-8:** *The Coming King*

• **Mark 9-16:** *The Servant King*

• **1 Peter:** *Living in the Real World*

• **Revelation 2-3:** *A Message from Jesus for the Church Today.* With *Jonathan Lamb*

thegoodbook
COMPANY

At The Good Book Company, we are dedicated to helping individual Christians and local churches grow. We believe that God's growth process always starts with hearing clearly what He has said to us through His timeless word—the Bible.

Ever since we started in 1991, we have been striving to produce resources that honour God in the way the Bible is used. We have grown to become an international provider of user-friendly resources to the Christian community, with believers of all backgrounds and denominations using our Bible studies, books, evangelistic resources, DVD-based courses and training courses.

We want to equip ordinary Christians to live for Christ day by day, and churches to grow in their knowledge of God, their love for one another, and the effectiveness of their outreach. Call us to discuss your needs, or visit your friendly neighbourhood website for more information on the resources and services we provide.

UK & Europe: www.thegoodbook.co.uk
N America: www.thegoodbook.com
Australia: www.thegoodbook.com.au
New Zealand: www.thegoodbook.co.nz

UK & Europe: 0333 123 0880
N America: 866 244 2165
Australia: (02) 6100 4211
New Zealand (+64) 3 343 1990